battle of
NORMANDY

Operation *Goodwood*
The 11th Armoured Division in action

Didier **LODIEU**

Drawings by Nicolas GOHIN — Maps by Antonin COLLET
Translated from the French by Alan Mckay

Histoire & Collections

We have to breakthrough

Since the landings in Normandy, the Allies had enlarged their bridgehead and were driving slowly inland into the heart of Normandy. This advance was much slower however that the General Staff had planned. Indeed the Germans were putting up a fierce fight and Anglo-Canadian losses were heavy. In order to widen the bridgehead, Montgomery launched another offensive.

To the east of the River Orne and to the north of Caen, the British 21st Army Group held a bridgehead called the "Colombelles Triangle". This sector had been held since the days following the landings on 6 June 1944. It was a

Above.
The most battle-hardened unit that the 11th Armoured Division had to face in the first hours of the offensive was the Pz.Gren.Rgt. 125 under Oberst von Luck, a unit under the responsibility of the 21. Pz.Div. On 1 June 1944 this division had a total strength of 16242 officers and men; by the 1 July there were 13245 left; on the 1 August it rose back up to 14850 men, this last figure being explained by the fact that marching battalions had reinforced it. According to a report dated 7 September 1944, the division could then only line up a maximum of between six and eight thousand men, no tanks, one or two Sturmgeschütze, three to five 105 mm field howitzers, four heavy howitzers, two 88 mm Flak guns, and from five to ten SPWs. 60% of its vehicles were light vehicles and 30% trucks.
(BA 101 I / 493/3365/26)

sector roughly 3 miles by 5 (5 km by 8), which each successive unit engaged there had not yet succeeded in enlarging. The German LXXXVI A.K. soldiers had not yet yielded a single yard of ground in spite of repeated British attacks. Field-Marshall Montgomery wanted to break this strong opposition and open up the road to Falaise by launching an offensive called *"Goodwood"*. But before this town was reached (in the end it was liberated only on 15 August 1944!), the British VIIIth Corps had to break through the 16.FeldDiv. (L) and the 21.Pz.Div. lines which were staggered up to the Caen-Vimont railway line, before pushing on southwards.

Because the bridgehead was so small Montgomery and his staff could only get one regiment at a time to attack frontally. They decided that the 11th Armoured division (11th Armd. Div.) would open the way with the other divisions following.

When the VIIIth Corps CO, O'Connor, talked to the 11th Armd. Div. CO, Major-General Pip Roberts, he informed him that his division was going to be the operation's fer-de-lance.

Two other armoured divisions were to follow his unit once it had progressed far enough through the enemy lines. The second was to be the Guards and the last, the 7th Armd. Div., the famous *"Desert Rats"*. The mission of Roberts' 11th Armd. Div.'s armoured punch, the 29th Armoured Brigade, was to capture the villages at Bras, Hubert-Folie and Fontenay to protect the right flank of the army corps. The division was to take Cagny as well as Cuverville and Démouville en route. Both these villages were to form the start line.

PIP ROBERTS' WORRIES

His superior's over-ambitious plan worried Major-General Pip Roberts. The conversation between the two men became tense. Roberts suggested that the 51st Highland Division, which was holding the Colombelle Triangle, attack Cuverville and Démouville. This would release its infantry brigade, the 159th, which could thereafter come to the aid of his armoured brigade which had to take Cagny on its left, clean out the villages situated in the centre then fall back on the right.

But O'Connor was confident his plan would work. He retorted that his armoured brigade's advance would be protected by eight (medium) field artillery regiments which would open up with a 2 000 yards wide artillery barrage advancing 15 yards a minute, 4 300 yards towards the south-east and 2 000 yards to the south-east.

The conversation ended when Roberts understood that he would not get O'Connor to change his mind. Not wanting to admit defeat, Major-General Roberts returned to his headquarters, rushed to his writing desk and repeated his request in writing, once again presenting the way he saw the plan. His request was soon on the VIIIth Army Corps' CO's desk.

Major-General Roberts recalls this episode in his memoirs: *"I learnt that the present plans could not be changed. I felt I had not been listened to and that I might be transferred to head another division at any moment. O'Connor asked me only to cover Cagny and not deal with it. I didn't really have any choice but to accept this situation, but I still think today that it was a stupid arrangement."*

On the eve of the offensive, Major-General Hobart, commanding the 79th Armd. Div. dropped in on Major-General Roberts. They had met at the beginning of the war when the latter was only an ordnance officer in the 6th Royal Tank Regiment.

Left.
Cap badge of the 23rd Hussars.

Below.
Although Major-General Roberts did not think they would, the AVRE or Crab Shermans turned out to be very useful during operation Goodwood, particularly when the Caen-Troarn railway line had to be crossed by infantry vehicles. They blew up the railway lines, breaching them so that the Bren Gun Carriers, half-tracks or other vehicles could get through. This one belongs to the 22nd Dragoons.
(IWM 3904)

After a few civilities, Hobart got to the point: *"I see you've not asked for any Flails."*

"No, Hobo, I haven't. There aren't any mines. The Germans have attacked this sector several times and they wouldn't have been able to if there'd been any mines. What's more, we don't want any of your vehicles cluttering up our line!"

Major-General Hobart insisted with his offer: *"My dear boy, nonsense, if you run into mines on the way the whole operation will fail and you'll look a damned fool. You'll have what? Some flail tanks but no mines! So what? Just remember that the flails can also be used as tanks!"*

In the end the old and the young generals compromised. One squadron of the Westminster Dragoons equipped with Churchill Flails would go with the 29th Armd. Brigade.

The bridgehead held by the 51st Highland Division was so narrow and situated in land so unsuited to deploying armour that the 11th Armd. Div. only moved up to the west bank of the Orne the night before the attack on 18 July 1944.

Realising that they were being watched by German spotters situated on the Bourguébus Crest, Major-General Roberts asked his officers to move around only if necessary.

OPERATION *"GOODWOOD"* PRELIMINARIES

Dawn was breaking when Major-General Roberts left his HQ to move to the heights from which he had

Above.
The tanks of the 3rd Royal Tank Regiment are assembling before dawn of 18 July 1944. At 5.45, with daybreak, the RAF bombers appeared in the sky. The bombs were dropped in sticks and then all hell was let loose on the German LXXXVI A.K.'s positions. The dense smoke seen here is rising from the enemy zone. Lieutenant-Colonel Silvertop of the 3rd Royal Tank Regiment is waiting for the start signal.
(Photo: Sergeant Laws IWM 3868)

a view of the whole of the enemy-occupied terrain; the Germans had no inkling that the first wave of bombers was about to appear overhead.

It was 5.45 by Roberts' watch when the Bomber Command machines came over. For 45 minutes, they went in one after the other laying what could only be called a carpet of bombs. At 07.00, 402 medium bombers of the 9th USAAF then followed dropping high explosive fragmentation bombs.

Major-General Roberts could not make anything out at all with the dust and the smoke caused by the bombs digging up the VIIIth Corps' next battlefield.

The 3rd Royal Tank Regiment tank crews finished their cigarettes, waiting for the bombardment by the 150-mm artillery guns and by the Royal Navy.

At 07.45, twenty-four heavy and eight medium artillery regiments unleashed a tempest of fire and steel with 600 guns (25 pounders) on the front line, held by the 16.Feld.Div.(L) Jäger. Most of these guns had remained west of the Orne because of the congestion inside the bridgehead to the east. The gunners set up an artillery barrage over a distance of 5 miles (8 km) from the 29th Armd. Brigade's start line.

Major-General Roberts, who was in his Tac HQ Tank fitted with two wireless sets, one for keeping in touch with his brigades and one for O'Connor's HQ, was ordered to launch his armoured brigade forward. The Military Police who were directing traffic dealt very well with this difficult task. Organisation and discipline prevailed.

Major-General Pips Roberts, leading the way in his tank, recalls: *"We reached some heights on the other side of the river, which had been used as the starting line for the artillery barrage. We moved ahead calmly. On our left I noticed the armoured brigade's tail units and on the right I could see our infantry brigade, the 159th, advancing in the direction of Cuverville. For the time being all was going well."*

Below.
A Sherman Firefly from the 5th Guards Armoured Brigade is rushing as fast as possible over "Buston" Bridge. The tank commander is wearing goggles which were quite indispensable because there was so much dust. There was even more of it once all the VIIIth Army Corps vehicles got moving on the battlefield.
(IWM 3884)

A report informed Major-General Roberts that the armoured brigade had been delayed crossing the Caen-Troarn railway line. Although the tanks managed well, the Churchill Flails and the Rifle Brigade half-tracks ran into difficulties.

Unfortunately, an incident held up the start of the operation. A minefield had been deliberately left in place by the 51st Highland Inf. Div. as a defence measure and the mines not removed. A Bren Gun Carrier drove into it and exploded. Miraculously the occupants got out unscathed. The sappers went in quickly to set up four passages, but the time spent doing so caused a traffic build-up which compromised the offensive.

Once the terrain had been cleared, the 29th Armd. Brigade left its start line in the following order: 3rd Royal Tank Regiment, 2nd Fife and Forfar Yeomanry and finally the 23rd Hussars.

A WALL OF ARTILLERY

The artillery barrage came up to within 200 yards of the 3rd Royal Tank Regiment's start line. The tankmen were frightened thinking their last moments had come and wondering whether the line of advancing fire would ever stop. A thick curtain of dust and smoke mixed with the explosions which shook the sector already pulverised by a deluge of shells.

The inevitable happened. William Moore of A Squadron recalls: *"Our own shells started falling among our tanks. Somebody running to cover shouted "Lieutenant Pells has been hit, he's dead."* He was in command of one of the Troops. A sergeant immediately replaced him and his radio operator took over Pells' tank.

Major Peter Burr, commanding B Squadron, was also killed (Author's note: replaced by Jock

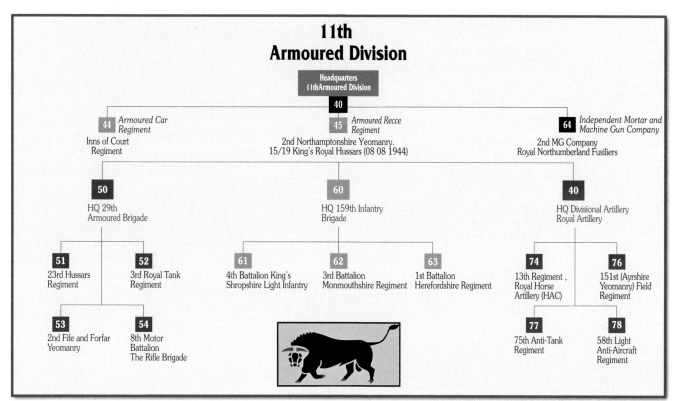

11th Armoured Division

Headquarters 11thArmoured Division

40

44 Armoured Car Regiment
Inns of Court Regiment

45 Armoured Recce Regiment
2nd Northamptonshire Yeomanry.
15/19 King's Royal Hussars (08 08 1944)

64 Independent Mortar and Machine Gun Company
2nd MG Company
Royal Northumberland Fusiliers

50 HQ 29th Armoured Brigade

60 HQ 159th Infantry Brigade

40 HQ Divisional Artillery Royal Artillery

51 23rd Hussars Regiment

52 3rd Royal Tank Regiment

61 4th Battalion King's Shropshire Light Infantry

62 3rd Battalion Monmouthshire Regiment

63 1st Battalion Herefordshire Regiment

74 13th Regiment, Royal Horse Artillery (HAC)

76 151st (Ayrshire Yeomanry) Field Regiment

53 2nd Fife and Forfar Yeomanry

54 8th Motor Battalion The Rifle Brigade

77 75th Anti-Tank Regiment

78 58th Light Anti-Aircraft Regiment

Balharrie); the situation remained confused for a while. Buck Kite, positioned on the right of A Squadron, did not understand why the tanks were turning round since the barrage was going away. Then I noticed the shells falling on our tanks. We lost about five COs, killed or wounded. Among them was Lieutenant Obaldeston. He had to be replaced at the head of his Troop. When we set off against the enemy we found we had lost one or two more tanks. The barrage approached to within a hundred yards of our leading tanks. It was now impossible to reorganise."

With the 23rd Hussars, the situation was scarcely better than the 3rd Tank Regiment's. This unit's association recorded: *"…then the Marauders suddenly appeared in the sky, shining brightly. Whistles and explosions in our sector attracted our attention. A bomb had fallen near 4 Troop of "B" Squadron, just as the unit's CO was talking to his men. Lieutenant Cochrane was seriously wounded and two tankmen were killed."* The first casualties were replaced by the LOBs (left out of battle = replacement personnel).

The Germans who had not yet got over the effects of the bombardment hardly had time to prepare their positions against the British. Many of them had already been killed by the artillery.

29th Armoured Brigade : Brigadier C. B. C. Harvey

3rd Royal Tank : Lieutenant-Colonel D. A. H. Silvertop MC

1 Squadron : Major Bill Rose
2 Squadron : Jack Balharrie
3 Squadron
Following the 19 July reorganisation, at 09.00 there were only two squadrons left :
1 Squadron : Major W. H. Close
2 Squadron : Major J. A. Watts

2nd Fife and Forfar Yeomanry : Lieutenant-Colonel Alex B. J. Scott

Second in Command : Major G. R. Totter
1 Squadron : Major Sir J. E. Gilmour
         Major A. W. A. Grant
         Major C. Nicholls (missing 18 July 1944)
         Major J. M. C. Powell (killed 19 July 1944))
2 Squadron : Captain J. D. Hutchinson
         Captain J. E. F. Miller
         Captain D. S. Mauch ou Manch
         Captain M. B. Melville
3 Squadron

23rd Hussars

A Squadron : Major Wigan
B Squadron : Captain Blackman
C Squadron : Major Shebbeare

8th Motor Battalion — Rifle Brigade : Colonel Tony Hunter

From 8.00 to 12.00:
The 29th Armoured Brigade's offensive

The British artillery barrage continued advancing towards the heart of the German positions whose occupants had to put up with this hellish fire. The 29th Armoured Brigade tanks, the fer-de-lance of the 11th Armoured Division, fell in behind this curtain of steel and fire.

Above.
A fascine-carrying Churchill of the 79th Armoured Division. Its canon has been replaced by a 90-mm mortar.
(IWM 3901)

THE 29TH ARMOURED BRIGADE logbook for 18 July 1944 – 08.00 records: *"The completely demoralised German soldiers surrendered in large numbers. Several of them left their positions and advanced towards the tanks with their hands up. They abandoned all their equipment. The combined onslaught of the bombers, the tanks and* *the artillery was too much for them."*

But the tank crews were not able to look after these stunned and tottering prisoners. Some of them had their eardrums burst by the thunder of the explosions; with a nod of the head or a wave of the hand, the tank commanders made them understand that they had to surrender to the infantry coming up behind them. Completely overwhelmed by the situation, the crew of an assault gun of the StuG. Abt. 200, trying to repair the barrel of their vehicle did not even realise that the 3rd RTR's tanks were upon them. They did not even hear them and were captured without any difficulty.

Corporal Jackson of C Squadron of the 23rd Hussars who was waiting desperately for a breakdown vehicle to pull his tank out of a bomb crater, captured 20 Germans with his crew. The crew found perfume and women's clothes in their trenches or foxholes. A medic in the regimental first aid post was so drunk he could not stand up.

THE GERMANS ARE STILL THERE

But the LXXXVI A.K. soldiers were far from all being drunk. Overall the Jäger of the 16.FeldDiv. and the Panzergrenadiere of the 21. Pz.Div. really started to fight from 10.00 onwards, at about the time they had more or less got over the successive poundings. VIIIth Corps reported widespread machine gun and Pak resistance in the middle of the morning.

At 8.40, the artillery barrage, which stopped on the south side of the Caen-Troarn railway line, enabled the Fife and Forfar Yeomanry to cross it and then deploy to the left of the 3rd Royal Tank Regiment (3rd RTR).

William Moore, a veteran of A Squadron of the 3rd RTR evokes his battalion's very technical organisation: *"It was organised into three waves. My own Squadron was on the right with "B" on the left, two Troops of four tanks each advanced in front: two were placed behind and the HQ Squadron with three Shermans was located in the middle.*

The second wave comprised the Battalion Commander with two HQ Shermans, 12 Honeys and a Recce Troop, two Flail Shermans which dealt with the mines, two armoured breakdown vehicles and a Carrier section of the Rifle Brigade.

The third wave was led by C Squadron and a battery of the RHA, self-propelled 25-pounders and the rest of Noel Bell's Rifle Brigade Company.

The Rifle Brigade companies brought a considerable number of vehicles to the assembly area. Each was equipped with 19 Bren Gun Carriers (11 for the Reconnaissance Section), two carried 3-in mortars, and six towed the 6-pounder anti-tank guns. Fourteen half-tracks transported the infantry sections. Incredible as it may seem, this mass of tanks, carriers, half-tracks and guns moved all onto the terrain without attracting the attention of the enemy spotters!

The two leading squadrons of the 3rd RTR who were lined up side by side and the two half squadrons of the third squadron forming the flanks made up a sort of box containing the command vehicles and the infantry. The self-propelled guns were placed at the rear."

INITIAL CONQUESTS

At 08.45, further artillery barrages introduced the second phase of the offensive according to the plan but the 3rd RTR tanks, slowed down by the terrain, had great trouble keeping up with them.

Suddenly the German artillery opened fire on the left flank of the two armoured battalions of the 11th Armd. Div. which made up the attack's spearhead. Moreover the infantrymen of the 3rd Monmouthshire from the 159th Inf. Brigade were heading towards Cuverville at 09.00. A Squadron of the 2nd Northants Yeomanry (the 11th Armd. Div.'s reconnaissance regiment) was moving up with them.

Below.
A long column of the Rifle Brigade of the 29th Armoured Brigade at the beginning of the offensive. F Company operated with the 2nd Fife and Forfar Yeomanry, G Company with the 3rd Royal Tank Regiment and H Company with the 23rd Hussars. E Company remained behind the Rifle Brigade HQ. The Rifle Brigade left its departure line at 08.15. (IWM 3864)

At 09.12, the 2nd Fife and Forfar Yeomanry was only 800 yards from Cagny. Eight minutes later, its first tanks and those of the 3rd RTR reached the Caen-Vimont road. The artillery barrage was lifted. The tankmen took advantage of this to cross the Caen-Vimont railway line. Apart from shots coming from some heights situated to the north of Cuverville - rapidly reduced to silence by the 2nd Northants Yeomanry's A Squadron - according to the unit's logbook, the Tommies of the 3rd Battalion of the Monmouthshire Regiment (3 Mon) from the 159th Inf. Brigade ran into little resistance in Cuverville. A large number of German soldiers had been killed during the bombardment. The captured survivors belonged to the II./Jg.Rgt.46 whose mission had been to defend Cuverville and Démouville with the 13./Jg.Rgt. 32 (L) equipped with six 75-mm cannon and some 150-mm pieces. These units were under the 16. FeldDiv.(L). Some soldiers from the I./Pz.Gren. Rgt. 125 were also engaged with the Jäger.

Judging by the time taken to capture the village - from 10.00 to 14.30 - one can assume that German resistance was not broken that easily.

With Cuverville cleaned out, the men of the 3 Mon headed for Démouville, quite decided to have done with the II./Jg.Rgt. 45. (L). This village, hidden behind some heights, was situated half a mile to the south of the infantrymen's start line where they were joined by the Daimler Scour Cars and Staghounds from A and C Squadrons of the 2nd Northants Yeomanry. This unit's B and D Squadrons got into line on the left of the Cuverville-Démouville road, to the right of the infantrymen.

Above.
Two soldiers from Pz.Gren.Rgt 125 spontaneously surrendering to the 11th Armoured Division infantry. One of the English soldiers, in the foreground, is telling them to go to the rear. The soldier on the left has kept all his equipment – gas mask and belt to which his bread bag, mess tin and flask are attached. The tube down his thigh would seem to be the sheath for the spare machine gun barrel. His comrade, who has abandoned everything, has even opened his jacket to show that he is not hiding any weapons. In the background is the Caen-Troarn railway line.
(IWM 3866)

12

Above and right.
The tank losses were terrible for the s.Pz.Abt. 503 and the Pz.Rgt. 22 as a result of the bombardments. Here we see two Tigers from 3./s. Pz.Abt. 503 destroyed in the park at Manneville where this company's tanks had gathered; they were commanded by General von Rosen then a Lieutenant. He recalls[1]: "The Tigers had to be engaged immediately, but before that, they had to be cleared with spades. Trees had fallen on them. The track had almost disappeared. How were we to organise the company? This work was frequently put off because of the naval artillery which sent over 420-mm shells. At one moment I noticed a crater 18 to 24 feet deep only 15 yards from my tank! The Tiger could have been buried. I also noticed that the rear armour plate had been seriously deformed as if it had been hit by a shell. The shock had bent the radiator. To this day I still wonder what caused that. Whatever it was, my tank was out of action and I had to get hold of another one. Our situation became increasingly difficult to hold…"
(Photo and Collection Frédéric Dupuis)

1: Taken from "45 Tiger en Normandie" by the same author. These two photos are shown for the first time in a book. I would like to thank Mr Frédéric Deprun who entrusted them to me so that they could appear in our study. It makes a change from the usual Tiger "313"!

THE FIGHTING FOR DÉMOUVILLE

Major Howe evokes this attack on Démouville: *"The soldiers were ordered to advance. They got up and started off through the wheat fields. They had only covered a few hundred yards when they came under fire from machines guns in the forward positions. The section leaders gained ground and these obstacles were rapidly eliminated; they then sent the groups of prisoners to the rear; resistance was encountered in isolated farms and in the fields approaching the village, but this was quickly reduced and more prisoners were sent to the rear."*

Fighting continued in the streets of Démouville; snipers lying in ambush in the church tower slowed down the infantry's progress. A large number of enemy soldiers retreated across the fields towards Giberville.

During this engagement C Squadron of the 2nd Northants Yeomanry destroyed two 105-mm assault guns from the Stug. Abt. 200 under Major Becker.

During the fighting, B Squadron eliminated the resistance points set up to the south of Démouville then was ordered to test the Giberville defences where once again it spotted Major Becker's terrible assault guns.

Behind Démouville the crew of a Carrier from H Company of the Rifle Brigade was put in charge of guarding the prisoners; suddenly their attention was drawn by German activity in some woods. Boldly a machine gunner sent several bursts of the Bren Gun at the woods and a few minutes later, 75 soldiers came out to surrender to the four men in the Carrier.

Major-General Roberts was worried and asked for the second phase of the artillery barrage to be delayed. He recalls: "The CRA dealt with organising this change while we were being seriously bombarded. Not being able to locate where this shooting was coming from I covered 500 yards with the Tac HQ to get under cover. When we got to where I

Above.
Three tanks from the 3rd Royal Tank Regiment advancing in formation across a wheat-field. They kept at a safe distance from each other. Here they are heading for the Caen-Troarn railway line. For the moment, these tanks have not yet been fired at by the enemy artillery or anti-tank guns. The scene is therefore taking place before 08.45.
(IWM 3877)

14

wanted to be we again came under fire. The map which was placed on a table and which the CRA was examining to do his calculations was cut in two by shrapnel. We had to get away from these heights; we went to a plateau lower down where the last of the armoured brigade tanks were struggling to cross over the old railway line. I must say that the APIS (aerial map section) had announced that the line could be crossed by our vehicles. It was the only mistake they made during the campaign."

Major-General Roberts met Brigadier Harvey in a wooded area in front of le Mesnil-Frémentel, a ruined village situated about half a mile from Cagny. The area which Harvey was occupying was being bombarded by mortar shells and the Flail Churchills were targeted by artillery pieces situated at le Mesnil-Frémentel.

The tanks of the 29th Armd. Brigade now advanced across devastated countryside over a distance

of some three and a half miles. The trees were broken, uprooted, the houses destroyed and the air putrid with the smell of dead cattle. But these nightmarish visions were not the only ones awaiting Roberts' tankmen; there were also the German infantrymen who started to emerge from their hideouts, ready to sell their skins dearly to stop the British troops.

The tanks of the 2nd Fife and Forfar Yeomanry advanced to the north of Démouville at 09.25. At the same time, the 23rd Hussars were only just starting to cross the Caen-Troarn railway line. The tank commanders had to be particularly careful because of the very deadly snipers lying in wait in the wheat fields or up in the trees.

As for the wheeled vehicles of the 159th Inf. Brigade, they advanced slowly. Their CO was only ordered to cross the Lirose-Démouville railway line at 10.45.

Above.
A and C Squadrons of the 2nd Northants Yeomanry support the infantry of the 3rd Mon for the attack on Démouville. One of the Daimlers in this reconnaissance regiment of the 11th Armd. Division has overturned into a ditch and is being immediately towed out by a half-track.
(IWM 3869)

15

As for the Guards Division, two armoured battalions of its 5th Guards Armd. Brigade carried on southwards, leaving Cagny on their right where the Coldstream Guards were engaged at 10.40. Passing le Mesnil-Frémentel, the 3rd RTR crews moved on in the direction of Grentheville. Fear gripped their guts. Their flanks were completely exposed. Major Bill Close commanding A Squadron, told his men to shoot at anything which moved. They got within sight of Grentheville at 09.36 and were taken on by the Nebelwerfer Rgt. 14's rockets, by 3./StuG.Abt. 200's assault guns and by a few of the Heer Pak Artillerie Abteilung 1053's Pak 75s.

Major Bill Close remembers: *"From my turret I could see the German artillerymen pointing their barrels in our direction. The Nebelwerfer missiles screamed over us. There were between 20 and 30 pieces located in the wheat fields facing the village. I ordered my tank commanders to shoot at them with their machine guns or to crush them with the tank tracks."*

The tankmen responded with their 75-mms, aiming at the positions the shooting was supposed to be coming from. The first tanks in A and B Squadrons were taken as targets. Like a steel forest marching forward, they drove on inexorably

Right.
This radio operator equipped with a Wireless Set N°38 is near an armoured vehicle of the Rifle Brigade studying where the enemy is on a map before calling in the Royal Artillery.
(IWM 3914)

Below.
Sappers clearing the railway of mines placed there by the Germans. Near them a Sherman has just fired in the direction of le Prieuré where Major Becker's Sturmgeschütze are situated. In the background is the Lirose level crossing house.
(IWM 3875)

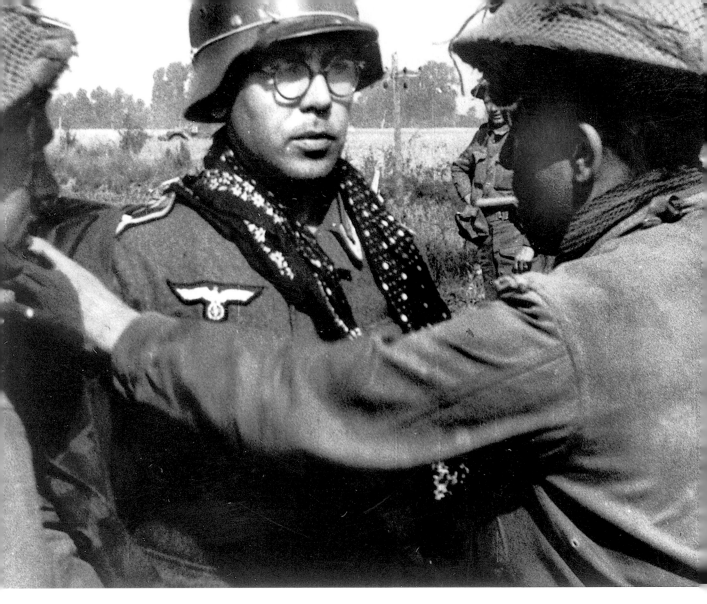

Above.
Near the Lirose level crossing house is a Pz.Jg.Abt. 16 (L) Pak position which has been destroyed by the 29th Armd. Brigade. An NCO from the German unit has been captured by men of the 11th Armd. Div. He is being properly searched. His Soldbuch (pay book) will be used by the intelligence service to identify the unit which was engaged. As can be seen, this Unteroffizier of the 16th Luftwaffe Field Division is wearing a Heer uniform and a Luftwaffe camouflage jacket which is being taken off him. It is most likely that his helmet also comes from the Heer but with a Luftwaffe eagle. Several items found in the region confirm this supposition. These details were particular to the 16th Luftwaffe Felddivision (L).
(IWM 3876)

towards the village. Their guns thundered. Shells whistled on all sides

However A Squadron, remaining behind suffered some losses. Major Bill Close recalls: *"Suddenly a Sherman on my left coughed out curls of smoke and stopped abruptly. Immediately every tank in the squadron turned its guns towards the village houses from which the shot had been fired. I noticed considerable activity near the trees in the orchards and the flashes from the anti-tank guns situated in the hedgerows surrounding the field. Two tanks from the Reconnaissance Troop were hit. The hatches opened up and the crews spilled out, throwing themselves to the ground and rolling over and over to smother their burning uniforms. The wheat field caught fire.*

The concentrated fire from my Shermans fell upon our attackers and we destroyed three or four of their anti-tank guns, killing the servers." It is quite likely that these tanks were destroyed by some of 4./ StuG. Abt. 200's assault guns which had remained in le Mesnil-Frémentel. Their crews had been ordered

by their Kdr., Hauptmann Ropke, not to move until the 3rd RTR tanks had gone past them and then open fire on their rear.

William Moore from A Squadron of the 3rd RTR also mentions the attack on Grentheville: *"I reached a small wheat field a few hundred yards from Grentheville when anti-tank guns (Heeres Artillerie-Pak-Abteilung 1 053 and StuG.Abt. 200) located on the edge of the village, opened up at us. Several shells came from some bushes and thickets and even from some farms. In a few minutes half a dozen of our tanks had been destroyed."*

Major Bill Close ordered his A Squadron crews to fall back on the railway line whilst firing high fragmentation shells at Grentheville. They came under very heavy artillery fire from this village while they broke off the encounter.

Before they got back to the railway line two more tanks were destroyed. Close reports: *"The tank of Buck Kite, commanding one of the Troops, engaged the enemy with his 17-pounder and smashed two anti-tank guns. Shortly afterwards he radioed that the shells from his tank had destroyed and burnt two assault guns.*

We suffered heavy casualties - seven tanks in my Squadron were destroyed. B and C Squadrons deplored the loss of a similar number of tanks."

As if by a miracle the A Squadron tank crews came across a tunnel under the railway embankment. It was not mined so William Moore carried out a reconnaissance at great danger to himself. He discovered magnificent, calm countryside and moved on. He

Above.
Not far from Lirose, a Sherman Firefly from the 23rd Hussars, like a watchdog, is guarding the Caen-Troarn railway line (not visible here) and waiting for its battalion's tanks to come up. Soldiers aboard a Carrier of the 8th Motor Battalion are hunting out enemy resistance points.
(IWM 3878)

(Continued on page 22)

This panorama shows us several tanks of the 2nd Grenadier Guards passing through the mine-cleared corridor where there are still some smoking wrecks of 11th Armoured Division tanks. As the Shermans advanced their crews came across countryside covered in thick dust, dense hedges and lines of trees reducing their vision. The tank commanders are searching for the enemy with their binoculars. The first three tanks which fell victim to the Paks were Shermans of B Squadron. This shot was probably taken at around 11.00 when Lieutenant-Colonel J.N. Moore asked his tankmen to make a brief halt following the failure of Major Sir Arthur Grant's attack on Cagny.
(IWM 3894, 3896, 3895)

21

(Continued from page 19)

carried on advancing along a line of hedges which led him as far as the factory at Cormelles. As he had not run into any opposition he contacted his squadron which quickly caught up with him.

Above.
This soldier from the Pz.Gre.Rgt. 125, a first machine gunner, has been photographed by the famous photographer-reporter of the 12.SS-Pz.Div. "Hitlerjugend", Woscidlo, in June 1944. The first battalion of this regiment was the unit in the 21.Pz.Div. which suffered the most losses on the morning of 18 July 1944. Indeed first it was in Bomber Command's bombardment zone, like 16.FeldDiv. (L) and then found itself along the line of attack of the 29th Armoured Division. Few of these men survived the war. The Heer camouflage jacket and the helmet cover were two items typically issued to the infantrymen in the 21. Pz. Div.
(Photo: Woscidlo)

UNDER FIRE FROM THE 88S

On the 3rd RTR's left, 300 yards from Cagny, 2nd Fife and Forfar Yeomanry's C Squadron came under terrible fire at 09.36. The first tank to brew up was the squadron CO's, Major Nicholl's. A bit later it was Captain J.E.F. Miller's, another Squadron CO, which was destroyed. In a few minutes 12 tanks were lost. 1 Battery of the 13th Royal Horse Artillery which was moving with the tanks also suffered heavy losses.

The 88-mm Flak battery (four guns) set up near Cagny cemetery and Heeres Artillerie-Pak-Abteilung 1039's anti-tank guns, lined up along the line of electricity pylons fired non-stop.

Being on a level with Grentheville, the 3rd Rotal Tank Regiment encountered strong resistance. They were shot at by Nebelwerfer, Sturmgeschütze and artillery. One of the crews is trying desperately to put out their burning Sherman.
(IWM 3867)

B Squadron of the 2nd Fife and Forfar Yeomanry which was responsible for protecting the flanks of the battalion now led the engagement.

"B and C Squadrons lost 12 tanks before the situation was got under control", the 2nd Fife and Forfar Yeomanry logbook reported.

A Squadron of the 2nd Fife and Forfar Yeomanry which comprised the first assault wave with B Squadron left le Mesnil-Frémentel on its right to reach the Caen-Vimont railway line. But it was ordered to stop because of the losses suffered by the other two squadrons further back.

As a result, the armoured battalion's CO, Lieutenant-Colonel Alex Scott who had organised an attack on Cagny in coordination with the 8th Rifle Brigade was ordered by Major-General Roberts to cancel this operation because of the squadrons' losses. To take up O'Connors' expression, Scott's tanks would just have to be happy "masking" Cagny.

THE WAY SOUTH-WESTWARDS IS BLOCKED

The stout defence of this village and the Guards Division being delayed getting to its position on the left wing of the 11th Armd. Div. at that particular moment, were the two major problems facing Major-General Roberts. He was quite unable to carry on south-westwards. The mortar fire continued. *It was all very intimidating,"* he recalls, *"but mortars or no*

mortars I had to reach Roscoe and work things out. Fortunately things were not going as badly as they seemed." Finally he sent the 2nd Fife and Forfar Yeomanry southwards in the direction of the Bourguébus-Frénouville line.

Major W. Steele Brownlie, commanding one of the squadrons of the 151st Field Regiment, a unit more commonly known as the Ayrshire Yeomanry also found himself in a critical situation when the 2nd Fife and Forfar Yeomanry suffered heavy losses near Cagny; He relates: *"Enemy mortar fire increased, but we nevertheless managed to cross the second railway line, my squadron's objective. My task consisted in watching our left flank while the 2nd Fife and Forfar Yeomanry moved up the valley. As I got into position a Sturmgeschütz opened fire on us and two tanks on my right started to smoke. We immediately engaged this self-propelled gun which we managed to destroy. It was at that moment that the 2nd Fife and Forfar Yeomanry's tanks were attacked. An entire Troop had been wiped out by the artillery pieces (Paks?) situated on our left flank in the woods. We destroyed three but some Panthers (Author's note: Pz.IVs or StuGs?) appeared on a hill. Things were getting worse. I destroyed one of them and my Corporal two but another one advancing on our left across the fields managed to cause some damage before we got rid of it.*

We asked our artillery to intervene, but they were too far behind us. I didn't have any precise idea of what had happened to the other units along the front, but there were tanks burning a bit all over the place and the number of burnt and wounded soldiers crawling everywhere in the wheat fields was frightening. We did what we could to help them but some died and others were killed by the shells which continued raining down on us; we started running out of ammunition at around midday."

Several tank commanders of the 3rd RTR, spotting smoke billowing from the 2nd Fife and Forfar Yeomanry's Shermans, told Lieutenant-Colonel Silvertop, their battalion CO. They were already starting to point their barrels in the direction of Cagny to help their comrades. But Silvertop forbade them to turn aside from their objective.

At 10.12, his Shermans were advancing southwestwards and his A Squadron which had crossed the railway line was heading south. It found itself very promptly engaged to the east of the railway line where it suffered losses from shots fired from both sides

Above.
Cap badge of the Royal Tank Regiment.

Left.
Shermans from the 3rd Royal Tank Regiment or from the 23rd Hussars pass Grentheville. The line of telegraph poles suggests they are about to cross the Départementale 613. The height of the wheat crop gives a good idea of how easy it was for the German soldiers to hide and fire at them without being seen. More than one Panzerfaust gunner was to set these fields on fire when he fired his missile which sent a large flame from the rear of the barrel.
(IWM 3916)

It was now the turn of the 23rd Hussars to face Grentheville. Their CO was waiting for intelligence from one of the three squadrons he had sent out to reconnoitre towards Four where the 2nd Fife and Forfar Yeomanry had just lost several tanks to a Panther and several anti-tank guns (at about 11.15). This Panzer had destroyed Alex Scott's tank before itself being destroyed by a Firefly.

The 23rd Hussars' crews were stupefied by the burning tanks near Cagny. The surviving crews headed back towards them on foot crossing the cereal fields their faces blackened from the smoke. The wounded with burnt faces and hands were helped along by those still unharmed. Some were carried on makeshift stretchers.

At 10.02, the 23rd Hussars' forward Squadron was recalled quickly because the battalion had to withdraw and face the Pz.IVs of the 21.Pz.Div.'s armoured regiment (Pz.Rgt.22) to the east of le Prieuré. Its new mission was to keep the road open for the Guards Armoured Division which was going

Below.
One of the SS-Sturmgeschütz Abt. 1 assault guns under SS-Hauptsturmführer Rettlinger destroyed at Tilly-la-Campagne a few days after Operation "Goodwood". This tank, like the others in the battalion, (except for the 3. Kp.), took part in the battle against the 23rd Hussars at the end of the afternoon of 18 July; the order which reached its Kdr. (at 15.00) was for him to lead his companies towards Bras and Ifs to join up with the I./SS-Pz.Rgt.1 assembled in the Hubert-Folie sector. After Operation "Goodwood", there were only 3 operational Sturmgeschütze left but on 1 August 1944, this battalion was back up to 23 Sturmgeschütze out of the 45 engaged on the first day.
(Photo: Briois. Coll., M. Dutheil)

Shermans of the 2nd Fife and Forfar Yeomanry waiting for the arrival of the 3rd Royal Tank Regiment before heading off towards Cagny where hell was waiting for them.
(IWM 3883)

Above.

A battery of Sextons from the 13th or 153rd Field Regiment pounding Grentheville to cover the advance of the Rifle Brigade. This self-propelled gun on a Canadian tank chassis with its 25-pounder gun equipped all the Field Artillery Regiments in the British armoured divisions.
(IWM 3920)

to attack Cagny in ten minutes. In fact they were faced with Major Becker's assault guns which after a short engagement fell back on le Poirier.

One of the 23rd Hussars' Squadrons was sent to the rear towards le Mesnil-Frémentel to attract the attention of the Germans entrenched in Cagny located on its right while its tanks waited out of range of the enemy artillery.

Le Mesnil-Frémentel had to be taken. Situated to the northwest of Cagny this village was along the main axis of the attack of 29th Armd. Brigade which had given it a wide berth. Although it had been destroyed by the bombardments, the Germans there still had some fight left in them. Several assault guns from the StuG.Abt. 200 had engaged the 3rd RTR

tanks and destroyed three of them. Soldiers from the Pz.Gren.Rgt 125 were also entrenched in the ruins. The village's defenders would hinder the armoured brigade's advance if not eliminated.

Noticing this threat Brigadier Roscoe Harvey ordered the Rifle Brigade to take the village. A tactical group was made up to carry out this mission and given to Lieutenant-Colonel Tony Hunter who got the support of some Churchill Flails of the 22nd Dragoons covering the assault carried out by a machine gun section aboard Bren Gun Carriers, AVREs and an anti-tank battery.

When the attack started, the Panzergrenadiere saw hordes of machines coming at them from all sides shooting at a hellish rate. The Carriers got into the burning village, driving over the heaps of smoking

rubble blocking the streets, smashed by the bombardment. Hauptmann Ropke's Sturmgeschütze crews could not hold on any longer. They high-footed it towards Four leaving the defence of le Mesnil-Frémentel to the infantry. Caught in the fire from Lieutenant-Colonel Hunter's tactical group and having no means of transport to escape with, the Panzergrenadiere could only fight; but they very quickly realised that they were sacrificing themselves for nothing and almost 130 of them allowed themselves to be captured.

According to the 3rd Inf. Div.'s log book, Hunter's infantry discovered several Panzer IVs in the village that had been destroyed during the bombardment. They belonged mainly to the 4./Pz.Rgt.22.

TAKING HUBERT-FOLIE

There was a problem: the reinforcements were in fact confined and bottled up within the corridor

used earlier by the 5th and the 29th Armd. Brigade tanks. These units were required to deploy as fast as possible in order to be able to manoeuvre and engage the enemy positions.

At 10.58, the tanks of the 3rd RTR were in sight of Hubert-Folie. From their turrets, the tankmen could see the outskirts of Caen. Their CO, Lieutenant-Colonel D.A.H. Silvertop, called in the artillery to soften up the village's defences before attacking. For the time being he did not know that there were several StuG.Abt. 200 assault guns, survivors from the fighting at Cuverville, set up there.

After an intensive pounding, he sent a section of Carriers forward under Lieutenant Stilemann to reconnoitre. As soon as they had moved forward, the self-propelled guns of the 13th RHA opened fire on the village.

The Carriers disappeared into the smoke towards the village and then came back shortly afterwards.

Above.
A Sherman of C Squadron from the 3rd Royal Tank Regiment is crossing the Caen-Vimont railway line. The scene took place between 10.00 and 11.00.
(IWM 3881)

30

Right.
During the 3rd RTR's advance, the tank crews came across this destroyed German artillery tractor with its 88-mm Pak to the south of the Caen-Vimont railway line. It seems likely that it was hit while being moved.
(IWM 3882)

Right.
One of the first tanks in the 2nd Fife and Forfar Yeomanry to be hit near Cagny between 09.36 and 9.45. In all twelve were destroyed. It is possible that it was the four 88-mm Flak guns under "von Luck" which destroyed these tanks, but no official claims support this idea. Other heavy vehicles like Becker's self-propelled guns and the 88-mm Paks from Heeres-Pak Abt 1039 were also present in the sector. The only proof which supports this idea is the official document which relates the death of Hauptmann Witzell in this zone and the destruction of 35 British tanks by his battalion.
(IWM 3870)

Incredible as it may seem, Lieutenant Stilemann signalled shortly afterwards that there were no enemy soldiers in the village.

William Moore from A Squadron did not agree as he found at a certain cost to his unit. He recalls: *"We found ourselves a few hundred yards from the nearest buildings when a heavy anti-tank gun opened up. I lost four tanks. My own tank took a direct hit. I heard someone shout 'Bale out, sir!' Once out on the ground I noticed that the shell had split the track in two near the rear. The shell could have been fired from Bourguébus which was only 2 500 m away. I ordered my commanders to turn back and shelter in the lee of the railway track then* went and joined the two Squadron HQ tanks. One had been destroyed but the other was intact (…) I got the Squadron under control again.

The rest of my battalion was engaged on my left. Seven tanks were burning. The crews who had managed to get out of those wrecks were trying to reach the railway. Several assault guns were spotted to the northeast of Bras as well as some armour, probably Panthers. The Pak and other artillery gunners continued spraying the sector.

We started a move towards Bras which was on a hill, near a wood. On the way I destroyed two assault guns and a Panzer before the tank on my left exploded. The crew got out and clambered onto my tank

helping the machine gunner, Hummer, who was a member of my peace-time football team. When I saw him, I thought: "My God, Hummer, you'll never be our goalkeeper again." Both his legs were only held by the tendons. As his mates placed him on the rear of the tank, I handed them the morphine. Hummer must have been holding something when the shell entered the tank because one of his hands had vanished and the other was all black. I decided to get him evacuated and called my medical officer.

A short while later a half-track came and picked him up. Unfortunately he died in hospital. I returned to the hill which had cost us so dearly. My tank was hit once or twice but was not destroyed…"

It was obvious that the German gunners set up between Bras and Soliers had spotted the 3rd RTR tanks as soon as they had come out of the tunnel and had just let them move forward. They had got themselves organised by radio, selecting their targets, then had waited until their guns were within range before opening up all at the same time, or almost, on the 3rd RTR's flanks.

Below.
Shermans belonging to the 23rd Hussars advance towards Grentheville after having crossed a line of trees. They are about to join up with the Rifle Brigade soldiers.
(IWM 3897)

Encouraged by the action of a Sherman which destroyed two Paks positioned in a forward position near Bras, A Squadron's tanks rushed off again towards the heights while Johnny Langdon's Troop tried to pass between Bras and Hubert-Folie. When they reached the road which linked the two villages, two tanks were hit but the two crews got out with only a few bruises.

As they moved forward, the 3rd RTR tanks suffered heavier and heavier casualties. To advance any further was suicidal. Lieutenant-Colonel Silvertop ordered his men to withdraw but still fire back. Meanwhile the 2nd Northants Yeomanry's B Squadron, ordered to join the 3rd RTR, had star-ted to cross the railway line when shots from two Sturmgeschütze destroyed two of its tanks. These assault guns were cleverly hidden in the factory at Cormelles.

It was difficult for the crews to deal with those StuGs because they risked being diverted from their objective if they tried to destroy them. The Squadron CO ordered smoke bombs to be fired to protect them while they crossed the railway line. Very quickly the scouts discovered the still-smoking wrecks of 3rd RTR tanks which made them go more carefully. C Squadron was sent up in reinforcement before the advance continued.

Still with no word from 3rd RTR, the crews moved across totally open ground southwards. They arrived in sight of Bras and Hubert-Folie. Here Paks and Panzers had set up "perfect positions" (the term used in the logbook) which enabled them to catch them in a crossfire at the ideal range. After losing several tanks, both Squadrons turned back.

THE DESERT RATS IN QUESTION

On the left of the 3rd RTR, the 2nd Fife and Forfar Yeomanry came closer to Bourguébus and its crest.

The unit everybody was waiting for - the 7th Armoured Division - should have already been engaged. At about 11.30, Roberts met its CO in the following circumstances. *"Suddenly I spotted Brigadier "Looney" Hinde, commanding the 22nd Ar-* moured Brigade of the 7th Armoured Division. He was out reconnoitring. On seeing him I guessed that the 7th Armd. Div was going to take over the sector between the Guards' and ours. Not a bit of it. When he turned up, he told me: 'There are too many enemy tanks here ready to welcome us. I am not prepared to engage my armour in that direction.' I was flabbergasted. Before I could explain that the tanks he had seen had already been destroyed,

Below.
One of the rare shots showing the deployment of the Rifle Brigade companies on 18 July 1944. Carriers and self-propelled anti-tanks guns can be seen here. According to Sergeant Laws, the infantrymen are progressing towards Grentheville.
(IWM 3917)

35

Above.
An Achilles tank destroyer of the 21st anti-Tank Regiment of the Royal Artillery. This tank buster equipped with a 17-pounder (76.2-mm) gun turned out to be indispensable against the Panthers and Tigers during the Battle of Normandy. Its shells were capable of piercing the 90-mm armour from 900 yards under a 30° angle of attack.
(IWM 3874)

Opposite page.
Sitting next to his foxhole, this Panzergrenadier from the 21. Pz. Div. is looking at the photographer in rather a relaxed manner. In the background we can recognise the chassis of a Panzer III, but the vehicle is difficult to identify because of the foliage covering it. It could also be a self-propelled gun.
(Photo: Woscidlo)

he had disappeared. I can assure you that the 7th Armd. Div. did not appear before 17.00. Some stories persist in saying that the Desert Rats had not been able to get through Cuverville and Démouville, but it seems they did not take the same route as our division and the Guards Division did. And yet, "Looney" must have taken the same route - there was no other."

There exists another, much less biting, report than Roberts', apropos the 7th Armd. Div.: *"The south could not be taken by the 7th Armd. Div. because it was held up behind the Guards Division. As it had not yet crossed the Orne, its armoured brigade put the 29th Armd. Brigade in a critical position because it was incapable of advancing."*

OBERLEUTNANT OEMLER'S TIGERS

Just as the 23rd Hussars' CO received the order from Brigade HQ to face a counter-attack

According to Sergeant Laws, this Sherman of the
29th Armoured Brigade was destroyed by an 88-mm
shell. By mid-morning on 18 July, 3rd RTR seemed to
have reached its objectives but the Germans had massed
Flak guns, artillery pieces, some Paks and Panthers to
the south between Bras and Soliers. The fighting became
harder and harder and British losses rose dramatically.
(IWM 3915)

Opposite page.
Cap badge of the Fife and Forfar Yeomanry.

by some Tigers on his left flank, a Sherman from one of the forward squadrons took a direct hit. The veterans from the 23rd Hussars recall: *"Suddenly the detonation from an 88-mm canon echoed in our ears. A Tiger was getting close across open ground coming from the east. It was with several other tanks…"*

It was exactly 11.38 when the 23rd Hussars tanks were engaged to the north-east of Cagny by the Panzergruppe under Oberleutnant Oemler who had just come round Emiéville by the east. This young Heer officer who was in command of the 1./s.Pz.Abt.503 had gathered four tanks together to launch a counter-attack on Démouville. He had two or three Tigers from his own company and one or two Pz.IVs from the Pz.Rgt.22. and they were probably covered by anti-tank fire from the Heer-Artillerie-Pak Abteilung 1039.

"Monkey" Blacker from C Squadron under Bill Shebbeare found himself behind the tank which had just been hit. He recalls: *"I swung our tank's gun round to where the shot had come from. There was a dark forest on our left from which the Panzers were shooting. We opened fire at them then manoeuvred for a while … In the battle which followed, the second Troop of C Squadron destroyed two Panzers and a Nebelwerfer. Captain Hagger destroyed a Tiger. A Squadron lost two tanks before the engagement was over."* A brief report mentioned the destruction of a single Tiger and a Pak.

When the first Guards Armd. Div. tanks joined the 23rd Armd. Hussars fighting Panzergruppe Oemler, the latter were ordered to leave the Tigers to the Guards and to head for Grentheville.

Later the 23rd Hussars CO sent someone to examine the wrecks more closely - King Tigers, monsters weighing no less than 68 tonnes.

UNDER WAY TOWARDS BOURGUÉBUS

The men of the Rifle Brigade HQ Company, supported by a few Flails from the Westminster Dragoons, attacked le Mesnil-Frémenthel.

Concealed behind a hedge situated to the north-east of a wood, Major-General Roberts joined Brigadier Harvey; he recalls: *"Once we had stopped, I saw my aide de camp jump down from his tank and rush into a trench then come out again with a superb pair of German binoculars. I*

gathered that he had got over his mosquito bites and that he could therefore take over his duties again. As soon as the Guards Division started to arrive, I asked him to contact the 23rd Hussars for them to set off. Shortly afterwards, Alan Adair, the Guards Armoured Division CO, arrived. I talked with him briefly then he decided to carry out a reconnaissance. After a few minutes, I saw his tank return very quickly with the GSO2 firing smoke bombs behind them. Apparently two Germans hidden in a trench had opened fire with a Panzerfaust at Adair's tank. They missed of course but more Grenadiere popped up out of hiding although they did not do anything."

For their part, the tank men of the 29th Armd. Brigade were finding it increasingly difficult to progress southwards. Without knowing it they had started to run into the third line of defence which had suffered a lot less from the bombardment than the first two.

This line of defence ran from Cagny, through Frénouville, Four, Hubert-Folie and ended at Bras. The tanks were now moving over open ground within range of the German guns which were very accurate, guns like the 88-mm Flak, the 75-mm Pak and the 105 and 155 assault guns of StuG.Abt. 200 under Major Becker. Then there were also some Pz.IVs and Tigers and especially some Panthers from SS.Pz. Rgt. 1 which maintained an effective defence from the end of the morning onwards. The Waffen-SS from the II./SS-Pz.Gren.Rgt. 2 under SS-Sturm-bannführer Becker who had left the Garcelles-Secqueville sector were advancing to take over the Four-Soliers line.

At 11.38 the 2nd Fife and Forfar Yeomanry tankmen spotted the first houses in Bourguébus and then the Pz.Art. Rgt. 155 105-mm guns opened up on the Squadron situated on the battalion's flank. The Squadron was hit hard. It is quite likely that the Heeres-Küsten.Art.

Above.
One of the four trucks belonging to the administration platoon responsible for bringing up petrol for the armour and other vehicles. The 20-litre jerry-cans are loaded by hand, a taxing task for these soldiers.
(IWM 3903)

Right.
The railway line had to be cleared of mines by the Engineers before the VIIIth Corps tanks could cross it.
(IWM 3913)

Above.
The pilot of a Typhoon has just been shot down over Démouville. He belongs to the 247th Fighter-Bomber Squadron. All the fighters in this unit were ordered to give air support to the VIIIth Corps during operation Goodwood.
(IWM 3906)

Abt. 1 255 122-mm pieces located to the south of the Bourguébus-Frénouville line were active during this pounding.

Lieutenant-Colonel Alex B.J. Scott radioed the 29th Armd. Brigade CO to ask him whether he had to take Bourguébus or Frénouville. The response was immediate: *"Deal with Tilly-la-Campagne via Bourguébus. From now on Frénouville is the 5th Guards Armoured Brigade's objective."* (order given at 11.42).

Scott signalled the 29th Armd. Brig CO that assault guns of the StuG.Abt. 200 were falling back towards Frénouville (note drawn up at 11.52). The speed with which these guns operated got on Roberts' nerves. He was to admit after the war that they greatly influenced the evolution of the battle.

Scott's remaining armour bravely advanced towards the south-east of Bourguébus in the direction of Tilly. A radio call echoed in the ears of each crew: "Panthers coming from Tilly are hurrying to Bourguébus. Watch out..."

Scott asked his men to remain discreet because the enemy tank crews had not spotted them yet. He got in touch with the 29th Armd. Brigade's HQ who reassured him by promising

him immediate intervention by Typhoons. The liaison was made by an RAF officer with his own radio operators, sitting in a Marmon Herrington armoured car, with orders to guide the fighter pilots onto their targets. This was a Forward Air Control Post (FACP). This new arrangement enabled fighters to be in constant contact with the Brigade HQ.

Major-General Pips Roberts remembers: "A few minutes after the tanks reached the railway line and the RAF had got in touch with the FACP, the armoured vehicle received a direct hit. The RAF officer was seriously wounded (12.15) but the idea was repeated as

it turned out to be extremely effective. In the meantime we resorted to the artillery gunners who designated the targets with pink-coloured smoke bombs."

The air attack had to be put off because of the loss of that RAF officer. A Second-Lieutenant was ordered to replace him and he helped all day.

Above.
Our pilot has managed to land with his machine in a wheat field. Of late, the Hurricanes had given way to the Typhoons equipping 247 Squadron which carried out several sorties before the month of June 1944. After the 6th, it was ordered to destroy any enemy transport and artillery pieces and to help the ground forces. As of 27 June 1944, it operated from the aerodrome at Coulombs, in the Calvados.
(IWM 3905)

The first two Tiger IIs destroyed in the European Campaign were Tiger II "111" belonging to Lieutenant Schroeder (our photo) and Tiger II "101", from 1./s.Pz. Abt.503., one of the two destroyed by Captain Hagger of the 23rd Hussars. Tiger "122" destroyed by Lieutenant Gorman of the Guards Armoured Division was therefore the third and not the first as inscribed on the monument near Cagny.
(Photo: D. et P. Briois. Coll.: M. Dutheil)

Opposite page.
Lines of advance used by the 2nd Northants Yeomanry on 18 and 19 July 1944
(from the Royal Armoured Corps. Vol. X N°2)

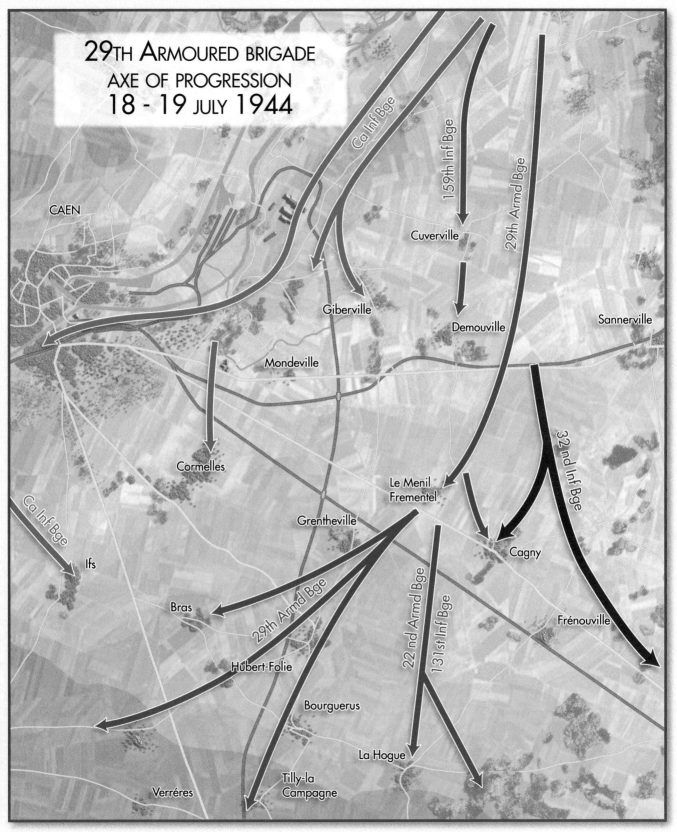

29TH ARMOURED BRIGADE
AXE OF PROGRESSION
18 - 19 JULY 1944

CAEN

Ca Inf Bge

159th Inf Bge

29th Armd Bge

Cuverville

Sannerville

Giberville

Demouville

Mondeville

32 nd Inf Bge

Cormelles

Le Menil
Frementel

Cagny

Ca Inf Bge

Grentheville

Ifs

29th Armd Bge

Frénouville

Bras

22 nd Armd Bge

131st Inf Bge

Hubert-Folie

Bourguerus

La Hogue

Verréres

Tilly-la
Campagne

From 12.00 until the end of the afteroon of 18 July:
The 29th Armoured Brigade offensive

Above.
This Panzer knocked out near Soliers is being examined by soldiers of the 1/5th Battalion, Queen's Regiment of the 7th Armoured Division. This division did in fact run into the I./SS-Pz.Rgt. 1 on 19 July (the shot was taken on the 20th) on both sides of Bourguébus.
(IWM 3929)

At 12.40, Lieutenant-Colonel Scott of the 2nd Fife and Forfar Yeomanry reported to Brigadier Harvey of the 29th Armd. Brigade that he only had 20 tanks in working condition left and that they were only 800 yards from Bourguébus. He was waiting for orders for the next stage of the operations.

THE BRIGADIER assured him that the tanks were being repaired and that it would not be long before they rejoined the remnants of his battalion. Indeed five of them turned up at Brigade HQ set up north of Grentheville and they were immediately sent to Scott (12.50). Brigadier Harvey asked Scott to clear out Soliers in his rear and leave Bourguébus alone because he considered it too dangerous for Scott's reduced strength. In the end this particular mission was given to the 23rd Hussars.

In the distance, black smoke billows from the burning
23rd Hussars Shermans who have just been hit by the
SS-Pz.Rgt. 1 Panthers at the beginning of the afternoon
of 18 July 1944.
(IWM 3909)

Right.
Sherman 1c Firefly
from C Squadron,
23rd Hussars,
11th Armoured Division

Above.
This German 1937 BMW car has burnt only partly because it was hit in the rear. Production of this four-wheel drive car began in 1933 initially for civilian use, but with the aim of eventually equipping the German army. It closely resembles the BMW G5. Most of them were made by Stoewer and Hanomag.
(IWM 3907)

In battle formation, B Squadron of the 2nd Fife and Forfar Yeomanry reached the first houses in Soliers and Four without running into any opposition. Two Troops from A Squadron under Captain Hutchinson covered the right flank. In a short exchange, their tanks destroyed two Panthers between Four and Poirier.

Unfortunately the 2nd Fife and Forfar Yeomanry's all-too meagre forces were slowed down in their dash by enemy infantry supported by eight Panthers from SS-Pz.Rgt. 1 who were in the Bourguébus sector. The two villages, Soliers and Four, were occupied by the Waffen-SS of the I./SS-Pz.Gren.Rgt. 1 and other Panthers which had been spotted earlier near Bourguébus. Other tanks were seen near a wood located not far from the 2nd Fife and Forfar Yeomanry. But this regiment had reached the limit of its capacities: it

had now lost too many tanks to do its job properly. O'Connor realised that Operation *"Goodwood"* had reached a stage where for the time being it was impossible to advance any further south. The traffic jam prevented the motorised infantry from supporting the armoured units properly as planned and as a result the offensive lost its impetus.

At 13.00 the 23rd Hussars' CO was ordered by Brigadier Harvey of the 29th Armd. Brigade, to clean out Bourguébus and move on to Tilly-la-Campagne. The 23rd Hussars' CO feared there might be a counter-attack from the southeast, judging by the number of Panthers spotted heading in that direction. Brigadier Harvey took his fears seriously because a few minutes later he contacted Colonel Hunter of the Rifle Brigade and asked him to place his troops southwest of le Mesnil-

Frémenthel and to set up defensive positions in preparation for a likely counter-attack.

To Lieutenant-Colonel Alex Scott's great relief, the 2nd Fife and Forfar Yeomanry's surviving crews suddenly saw Typhoons appear in the sky; they did not take long before flying over Bourguébus a second time. The pilots spotted ten Panthers and on their third fly-over at 13.30, rockets whistled from the wings of the aircraft down towards the Panzers. But the 88-mm Flak gunners realised the danger and opened up against these harbingers of death.

VON OBSFELDER COUNTER-ATTACKS

The Kdr of the LXXXVI. A.K., General der Infanterie von Obsfelder, realised that the two armoured battalions were using up their last strength against the heights situated south of the railway line. It was now up to him how the battle evolved. He decided to launch a counter-attack with the Panthers from the Four-Frénouville line. But before that, he had to gather together the rest of the armoured sections situated to the south of the railway line. Several movements were spotted, especially by the 3rd RTR which identified two Panzer IVs and some assault guns advancing towards Bourguébus, three Panthers approaching La Hogue, and nine other Panthers rushing towards Hubert-Folie. These latter were stopped in their tracks by Typhoons intervening aggressively. Three others were approaching Four.

While moving towards Bourguébus, at 14.07 the 23rd Hussars tanks were engaged by SS-Pz.Rgt. 1 Panthers. Four Shermans were quickly destroyed. The tank crews fell back a bit further to get into battle formation.

Suddenly three other Panthers escorted by two Sturmgeschütze attacked on one of the 23rd Hussars' battalion's flanks. Its CO was all the more concerned because he could see that the 2nd Fife and Forfar Yeomanry tanks were themselves in serious trouble. He was instructed by the 29th Armd. Brigade to get on the right flank of the 3rd RTR. He would thereby have a better chance of taking Soliers and Bourguébus. But the 23rd Hussars' CO retorted that he could not leave his positions because one of the 2nd Fife and Forfar Yeomanry Squadron Commanders had just signalled him that his unit would soon no longer exist, seeing the number of tanks lost. Naturally this report influenced the 23rd Hussars CO who was only thinking of saving his battalion, also engaged in a desperate fight.

At 14.45, the LXXXVI. A.K. launched its counter-attack against the 2nd Fife and Forfar Yeomanry tanks. Split into two groups, the Panthers moved quickly under cover of a smoke screen. The first group came from the west of Frénouville and the second attack was in the sector between Soliers and Bourguébus. Six Panthers, rapidly put out of action by the Shermans, were burning fiercely. The others nonetheless pushed home their attack.

The remnants of the 2nd Fife and Forfar Yeomanry were obliged to split up and engage in terrible tank battles which sometimes took place at point blank range in the vast wheat fields overlooked by the Bourguébus heights. The tank crews tried to be everywhere all at once to counter these Panthers turning up where they were least expected. Others remained hidden waiting for the right moment to catch them in their crossfire. It was

Right.
Cromwell Mark IV of the 11th Armoured Division HQ

The M10 Wolverines of the 11th Armoured Division played an important role during the offensive. Initially they gave vital support to the Rifle Brigade. Their 76.2-mm canon was a formidable adversary for the Pz.Rgt. 22 and the I./SS-Pz.Rgt. 1. This tank destroyer comes from a battery of the 75th Anti-Tank Regiment. (IWM 3865)

Right.
This Feldwebel from the Heer could belong to the Pz.Gren. Rgt. 125 or 192 of the 21. Pz. Div. The camouflaged tunic is typical of both regiments. His light yellow-painted helmet is camouflaged with blurred light green patches. He has placed chicken wire on top of his helmet. His trousers are also camouflaged and have been cut from tent canvas. They were made locally. These trousers as well as ten or so like them were found in the seventies near Vernon. They are in fact over-trousers. This Feldwebel is armed with a Panzerfaust 60, the terror of the 29th Armoured Brigade during Operation "Goodwood". (Reconstruction. © Militaria Magazine)

impossible to estimate the number of Panthers engaged because of the very thick white smoke caused by smoke bombs. The Shermans had to advance across totally open country.

Attacks followed counter-attacks one after the other. The German tank crews, the Panzerschützen, were experienced men. They sprung up, struck and disappeared again; they broke through hedges and jumped out behind the British. This nightmare lasted almost two hours. The left flank of the 2nd Fife and Forfar Yeomanry again came under fire from the

Paks and its losses increased dramatically. Several Shermans were hit.

Contact was lost with the Armoured Brigade HQ for more than an hour. Brigadier Harvey saw that the 2nd Fife and Forfar Yeomanry was in a bad way. As he should have heard from Lieutenant-Colonel Alex Scott, he asked the 23rd Hussars to go to his help. The tank crews crossed the railway line without no idea what the situation was really like. So the 23rd Hussars set off for Bourguébus.

"Monkey" Blacker of C Squadron recalls: *"We were advancing across the wheat fields in battle formation. A and B Squadrons were leading followed by the four HQ tanks, then C Squadron. We reached the railway line which we crossed easily then stopped for a minute. All the tank commanders had taken out their binoculars and were inspecting the steep slope leading up to the Bourguébus Crest about three miles away. A large number of tanks occupied the terrain and in the smoke it was impossible to tell friend*

from foe, dead or alive. "The 3rd RTR must be placed further forward", said Perry Harding to the Squadron Commanders, *"Move on and we'll find out what has happened to the Fifes. C squadron remain here in reserve.*

Half a mile further on, we caught up with the tail of the column of the 2nd Fife and Forfar Yeomanry.

Above.
Sheltering from the Allied pilots by hiding under a tree, officers from a Flak Abteilung HQ are studying their maps to decide on the best places for their batteries. All calibres of AA in the Flak Sturm-Regiment 2 under Oberst Moser which cost the VIIIth Corps' armour so dearly were positioned between the Bourguébus Crest and the Secqueville Wood, then on a line turning north-eastwards, crossing the Caen-Vimont railway line, up to Troarn.
(BA 101 I/494/3392/17)

Its tanks were right in the middle of open ground near the crest. What were they doing there?

Suddenly we realised that all these tanks had been destroyed and that the only signs of life were the wounded men, heading for the rear on foot. A reconnaissance vehicle turned up and ran into Perry's tank. In it there was a Squadron Commander from the 2nd Fife and Forfar Yeomanry, John Gilmour. He got out, bareheaded and his face blackened by all the smoke, and informed with the utmost calm: "I don't think that we have more than four tanks left. When our tanks and those of the 3rd RTR were near the crest, we got caught in the fire from the Panzers and the artillery situated up there. As you can see for yourself, there is no cover. So I was therefore on the qui-vive."

Facing us were two hamlets, Soliers and Four, now reduced to piles of rubble out of which some trees were sticking.

Suddenly we were attacked by some Germans who rushed out from the villages and the woods situated along the Bourguébus Crest. We came under withering fire, pinning us down in the bottom of a hollow. The range of the Shermans' 75-mm guns was insufficient. The long barrels of the Sherman Fireflies were easily spotted and were the enemy's priority targets."

THE 23RD HUSSARS IN THE STORM

Just as the tank 23rd Hussars crews were receiving this information, the 1st Troop tanks of B Squadron were hit and set ablaze in less than two minutes; the raucous barking of the Sturmgeschütze 75-mm guns could be heard. The other Shermans in B Squadron manoeuvred in the smell of hot oil and the crews started to respond, showering the enemy with a hail of shells.

During this confrontation, a Panther was seriously hit by the shells from Sergeant Bateman's tank and started to burn. The flames seemed to climb into the sky but Bateman did not have time to relish his victory: he was killed by a shell which pierced his turret. In a few minutes B Squadron had lost 16 Shermans. *"Captain Blackman also destroyed a Panther but in a minute, his tank had caught fire too"*, the 23rd Hussar veterans recall. They remember this black day very well. *"B Squadron then A Squadron, which fell back still firing, started losing tank after tank.*

Below.
PzKpfW IV Ausf. H from the 6th Company of the II./22. Pz. Rgt. of the 21. Pz.Div. The classic green over sand camouflage has been applied in the field and the numbers stencilled on.

The CO, sheltering inside the turret of his tank was talking to brigadier Harvey when a Panther attacked his tank. Fortunately the pointer, RSM Wass, scored a brilliant kill and eliminated this dangerous Panther. The last tanks and the HQ broke off seeking shelter behind the nearest hedge. But they were still within range of the Panthers and now in a desperate situation.

Most of the seventeen 75-mms were destroyed and the 6-pounders were practically ineffective in these circumstances. Every five minutes, armour piercing shells whistled through the air before piercing the Shermans' steel. First of all there were sparks, then flames covered the tank; in the end it became a dark silhouette against an incandescent orange glow while it was lifted off the ground for an instant. Sometimes we had the

time to save a wounded comrade. We could at once hear the cracks of the metal parts as they started to break apart while it burnt. Black smoke escaped from the turret and later at intervals, there were reddish flashes and violent rents as the ammunition exploded. But B Squadron continued to reply as it fell back, with A Squadron hurrying along on its right flank; this was to influence the outcome of the battle."

Although the Panthers were mentioned in all the logbooks and reports of the 23rd Hussars veterans, the SS-Sturmgeschütz Abt. I assault guns under SS-Hauptsturmführer Rettlinger also took part and have to be taken into account. They came up at around 17.00, having been ordered to attack at 15.00 with the 1.Kp in the Bras sector

and the 2. Kp to the north. These two companies had taken the 23rd Hussars' tanks in a pincer movement as they were moving towards the high ground. At that moment the tankmen had fired at the assault guns which immediately responded. *"Two of their tanks were set ablaze",* Rettlinger reported *and others were hit. The British started to panic. Several tanks tried to flee and find shelter. Even the enemy tanks situated near Hubert-Folie retired after we opened fire. When they broke off, they found themselves still under fire from the Sturmgeschütze of the 2. Kp who knocked out some more tanks. We did not lose a single tank. The fighting ended at around 19.00".*

The 29th Armoured Brigade's War Diary has recorded the following on this subject: *"At 14.45, B Squadron of the 23rd Hussars which was facing* Bourguébus was practically destroyed while the second (Author's note: C Squadron) was approaching Four. The battalion's third Squadron (A) was in a sorry state near Grentheville."*

"Monkey" Blacker of C Squadron recalls: *"Peter Harding who was inside his tank was talking with the Brigadier. He was quite unaware of what was going on around him. Suddenly a dull sound echoed. A geyser of earth sprang up less than ten yards from his tank. This was the moment for the regimental HQ to go into action. My Regimental-Sergeant-Major pushed an armour-piercing shell violently home into the breech then stared through the telescope waiting for my orders.*

Among the debris and the wrecks which littered the escarpment of the crest there were shapes

Below.
Servers of a 50-mm Flak 41 pushing their gun, using its running gear to get it in position in a field. The production of this model was rapidly stopped at the beginning of the conflict because it was thought to be unsatisfactory.
(BA 101 I/496/3495/29)

which could not be mistaken for anything else: Tigers and Panthers. A Panther was pointing its gun in our direction. This tank was really facing me, presenting armour which was too thick for my gun. It was this tank that had fired at Perry. "Traverse, right, ready…at 600 yards…Fire!"

I received what was like whiplash in my face while I was watching the target from the turret. At the moment when the mechanism recoil hit my knee and the empty shell fell on the floor I just had the time to see my shot hit its target in the centre. To my great surprise, I saw shadows leaving the wounded Panther which had been hit just where the turret joins the superstructure. A myriad of sparks showered forth: the tank had been hit at its most vulnerable point. Perry did not know what was going on. We fired smoke bombs to cover our slow retreat towards a hedge a few hundred yards further back.

The battle continued. Orders thundered out from the rear: *"Hurry up! The German reserves are rushing to the other parts of the front. Rush to the heights before they arrive. The Guards and the 7th Armoured have been delayed. Don't count on them for today. Forward!"*

But with the village of Four and Soliers still not taken and with the Bourguébus Crest alive with tanks and 88-mm Paks, this order was impossible to carry out, all the more so as the armoured force was seriously depleted.

C Squadron located somewhere behind some high ground on our left, now made up our division's only armoured reserve. Its CO was given a report about the seriousness of the situation and the urgent need to move forwards, if needs be paying the ultimate sacrifice. It had to get through to Four.

It is easy to be calm and disinterested after the battle; to forget how anguished you were in the turmoil, smoke and dust. In this fray it had become almost impossible from what you had seen to determine exactly where the enemy positions were on the map."

C SQUADRON'S DEATH THROES

23rd Hussars' C Squadron tank crews were on the left of B Squadron, positioned on a hill situated about 300 yards from Four. *"Suddenly without warning, the whole squadron was subjected to a terrible concentration of fire from Four, almost a point blank range"*, the veterans of the 23rd Hussars recall. *"No time to fire back, no time to do anything, just time to glance quickly at the situation. In less than a minute all the tanks of the three Troops and the HQ Squadron had been hit.*

From all sides, the wounded and the torch-like silhouettes ran or advanced with difficulty trying to get under cover while a hail of armour-piercing shells riddled the Shermans. Major Shebbeare's tank was one of the first to go up. We never saw him again. Stunned survivors rushed to help the wounded, hitting the burning uniforms with their hands until the intense heat and the violent explosions pushed them back to the railway line. Captain Walter was wounded in the hand by an armour-piercing shell as he was getting himself out of his tank. Despite this wound, he managed to get the wounded gathered together, to bring them to the rear and make sure they were cared for. He then clambered aboard a Firefly from which he reorganised the rest of the Squadron and destroyed per-

Previous page.
Hidden in a wood, some Luftwaffe mechanics have come to replace a damaged 88-mm canon. The gun's running gear is in the foreground. Because of the weight of the barrel, they definitely need a gantry crane.
(BA 101 I/497/3503A/27)

Right.
This Feldwebel is wearing the black uniform of the Panzertruppen and could belong to the Pz. Rgt. 21 of the 22 Pz.Div. when it was constituted in the first half of 1943. During the Battle of Normandy, many crewmen got rid of their woollen tunics which were much too warm for the season. They exchanged them for the same style of tunic but cut from a finer green cotton cloth, but because this article of clothing was relatively hard to come by, they wore the jackets belonging to the Heer uniforms after, of course, slipping on the Panzertruppen coloured shoulder flaps. Finally some even wore the rare green trousers with the left-hand thigh pocket. This Felwebel is wearing the standard cap which appeared in 1943 to replace the black forage cap (which was still around during the summer of 1944). The Feldwebel is also wearing the ribbon awarded for services in the rear (Verdienstkreuz), the bronze tank combat medal and the black medal for the wounded.
(Reconstitution. Photo Militaria Magazine)

sonally one Panther. He refused to be evacuated during the next 24 hours. He was later awarded the DSO. Sergeant Abott was awarded the Military Medal, "For returning to the fighting on foot and for searching for the wounded even though the terrain was occupied by the enemy and under fire."

According to "Monkey" Blacker's memoirs, the wrecks of 106 British tanks littered the Bourguébus Crest, as well as a considerable number of Panzers.

The remainder of B and C Squadrons of the 23rd Hussars fell back on the Caen-Vimont railway line without further ado. Meanwhile A Squadron took on the enemy dug in west of Grentheville, thus protecting the battalion's flank. Even though they were hardly in a comfortable position they did score a few hits, particularly in the village itself which sheltered some rather active German soldiers.

Likewise, Lieutenant-Colonel Silvertop, under fire from the anti-tank guns and artillery, broke off with his 3rd RTR tanks at the beginning of the afternoon. But his tanks very quickly stopped because they had run out of fuel and ammunition. Supply trucks were sent to them. This was a perilous mission for the lorry drivers who risked being hit at any moment. One by one the crews filled up and loaded as much ammunition as they could before continuing their withdrawal.

DEAD-END TOWARDS THE SOUTH

At 15.00, Lieutenant-Colonel Alex Scott of the 2nd Fife and Forfar Yeomanry was ordered to break off towards Grentheville then come and meet Brigadier Harvey of the 29th Armd. Brigade at his HQ set up at Cuverville. A few minutes later, all his tanks were to the north of the Vimont-Caen railway line and at 16.00 Scott turned up to meet the armoured brigade's CO.

Meanwhile the 5th Guards Armoured Brigade got hold of Cagny and started pushing southwards, towards Vimont. It also met strong resistance from the Germans south of the railway line.

The information gathered by O'Connors' HQ was not good enough. The situation was becoming very confused. The VIIIth Corps CO could not take any decision without the risk of making a mistake.

The RAF fighters fared no better than the Shermans against the Panthers who were liable to recover all the terrain VIIIth Corps had gained during the morning.

Further north the situation became catastrophic for the Rifle Brigade who were obliged to abandon Grentheville captured only a few hours earlier.

It was quite obvious that LXXXVI. A. K. was holding General O'Connor's VIIIth Corps at bay. It was impossible for 11th Armoured Division's three armoured battalions to break the German defences south of the Caen-Vimont railway. The element of surprise which constituted one of the trumps for the successful outcome of the offensive had simply withered away. When the 11th Armoured Division's situation is studied more closely, we find the 2nd Northants Yeomanry (which was part of the armoured brigade) placed to the west of the Caen-Vimont railway line, facing the enemy and the 3rd RTR located on a short line facing Bras and Hubert-Folie. The 23rd Hussars' tanks were placed as watchdogs in front of Grentheville – le Poirier and Four. As for the 2nd Fife and Forfar Yeomanry, in the process of being reorganised 2 000 yards to the north of Grentheville, it constituted the 29th Armoured Brigade's reserve.

Only an hour later the first elements of the 7th Armoured Division appeared in the la Hogue sector, south of Four. Meanwhile, the 159th Brigade, relieved by the 51st Highland Division, set off to establish solid positions on either side of le Mesnil-Frémentel.

AT THE END OF THE DAY, 18 JULY 1944

The three armoured battalions remained in their positions still in danger from the enemy artillery. Major-General Roberts knew perfectly well that his tanks could no longer advance against the enemy lines.

His crews were overcome by a feeling of defeat. The offensive had not worked out as planned and far too many soldiers had died trying to reach their objectives; and yet these had been within their grasp. These men had to be replaced urgently. During the night torn by tracer bullets and shells continually harassing 11th Armoured Division's worn-out soldiers, complete crews and specialists moved up.

In the 3rd RTR's logbook, it says that at 21.00 four Tigers attacked the battalion from high ground. The 2nd Northants Yeomanry came to its rescue. An hour later, it was three Tigers and some Panthers which opened fire on the tanks from another hill. At 22.15, six Shermans in the unit were destroyed. The unit retired and 12 of its tanks stood by to repel any further attacks.

"Following its tank losses, the 3rd RTR reorganised its three squadrons with only ten tanks each", says Bill Close, *"I was lucky that I still had my two experienced sergeants, Buck Kite and Freddie Dale. None of us was looking forward to the morning with any enthusiasm. The Bourguébus Crest with its strongly held villages was an objective which daunted our completely exhausted troops."*

To be precise, this reorganisation took place early the following morning, 19 July. A Squadron was commanded by Major W.M. Close and B Squadron by Major J.A. Watt. The crews and tanks of C Squadron were shared out among the other two squadrons.

Right.
"Some infantrymen from the 159th Brigade have just got hold of some cider in a farm which has been damaged by the artillery", Sergeant Grant says. The soldiers' features are haggard with fatigue and from the oppressive heat. Although they quench their thirst during this pause, they are still tense from what they have just been through and what they are about to go through. The bull's insignia is visible on the battledress of the man on the left.
(IWM 3924)

As Bill Close leads one to believe, his battalion losses were heavy, but they were for the 29th Armoured Brigade's other two battalions also. The 3rd Royal Tank Regiment had lost exactly 41 tanks, the 23rd Hussars had lost 26, the 2nd Fife and Forfar Yeomanry 43 and the 2nd Northants Yeomanry 16 (15 Cromwells and one 95-mm), i.e. 126 tanks lost in all.

The casualties for the 11th Armoured Division were 336 men. For the Guards Division they were 137 and for the 7th Armoured Division 48. Unfortunately not all the wounded were brought to the first aid posts which were completely overwhelmed. For example, Captain Mitchell himself alone looked after 70 soldiers whose terrible condition was an omen of worse things to come and it was impossible to evacuate all these wounded who were piling up in the Regimental Aid Post. Nobody knew clearly yet where the wounded still in the wheat fields were, and who they were. This was the only time in the whole of the Normandy Campaign that the medical personnel were overwhelmed by the number of casualties.

During the night Luftwaffe aircraft had a go at the bridges the Engineers had thrown across the Orne and over which the VIIIth Corps had crossed the previous day. But it was more frightening than anything else…None of the bridges was hit.

During the artillery barrage, Major Seymour of the 23rd Hussars was seriously wounded. It was Major Wigan who replaced him at the head of A Squadron. Some new tanks came up to replace some of those which had been destroyed during the day. The 23rd Hussars remained in their positions, in reserve, to the north of the railway line.

Left.
This Panther was destroyed on 18 or 19 July 1944 during operation "Goodwood". It belonged to the I./SS-Pz.Rgt. 1. On the eve of the offensive the battalion numbered 48 Panthers. Two days later its strength was reduced to 17, i.e. company strength. Nonetheless, the repair workshop mechanics managed to work miracles, since on 5 August 1944 43 Panthers were operational. It would seem that I./SS-Pz.Rgt. 1. was never at full Panther strength in Normandy. By consulting the number of Panthers available each day between 4 July and 5 August 1944, we see that the day when it had the greatest number of operational tanks was 17 July with 48. The following day, it only lost two. On the other hand between 19 and 20 July it lost 39 Panthers but was able to repair most of them for the offensive against Mortain.
(Photo: Briois. Coll., M. Dutheil)

19 july 1944
The second day of the offensive

Major-General Roberts had only had a few hours' sleep. Sitting in the rear of his command car examining a map of the region, he was waiting for his aide de camp to bring him a cup of coffee.

I T WAS IMPOSSIBLE for his two battalions to resume their offensive at dawn given the time needed to reorganise the 29th Brigade. Suddenly a shell exploding tore him from his thoughts. Nobody was wounded but his driver had spilt the coffee over Roberts' case!

At 12.00 there was a conference at Major-General Roberts' HQ. General O'Connor was present as were Generals Adair of the Guards Division and Erskine of the 7th Armoured Division. Together they set up the following plan for the day:
At 16.00, the 11th Armd. Div. would get hold of Bras, in spite of the 88s which covered the high ground. After that it would be the turn of Hubert-Folie.
At 17.00, the fresh 7th Armd. Div. would have the main job of the day: taking Soliers and Bourguébus.
At the same time, at 17.00, the Guards Armd. Div. would attack Poirier and advance in the direction of Frénouville.

Major-General Roberts had doubts about Erskine's support and wrote: *"It goes without saying that I asked Erskine if he'd do his best to reduce the defences in the Bourguébus sector while I attacked Bras and Hubert-Folie. Naturally he confirmed that he would follow orders. As for me, I promised I'd help him after I'd captured Bras and Hubert-Folie."*

As far as Major-General Roberts was concerned he was really relying more on the divisional infantry rather than on his diminished armoured brigade to lead the capture of Bras and Hubert-Folie. The tanks' action would be limited to supporting the 8th Motor Battalion which had to advance almost 3 000 yards across open ground before attacking. Once the infantry battalions had managed to advance that far, other battalions from the 159th Infantry

N°2 Company under Major M.J. Turnbull and N°4 Company under Major J.D.A Syrett launch an attack on le Poirier on 19 June 1944 at 05.00. They only ran into weak opposition: some Germans were captured and the others fled. Both companies of the 1st Battalion dug their own foxholes around the village. They remained there until 22 July 1944.
(IWM 3923)

Brigade would come up and assist them clearing out the captured villages.

A CAUTIOUS ADVANCE

At 16.00 the Rifle Brigade (8th Motor Battalion) soldiers advanced cautiously with the tanks through the wheat fields from which death could spring up at any moment. The three companies were placed under the command of Colonel Tony Hunter. At 03.00, they reached the Caen-Vimont railway line and then started crossing it an hour later. Only once the railway line was crossed did the motorised infantry come across the 2nd Northants Yeomanry

Above.
Major J.D.A. Syrett, commanding N°4 Company of the 1st Battalion of the Welsh Guards is pointing at a target for Sergeant J.A. Veysey who was in charge of a group of 3-in mortars. The soldier in the foreground is Guardsman G.S. Kitchen. Major John David Alfred Syrett was killed on 22 July 1944 aged 28. Today he rests in the cemetery at Banneville-la-Campagne.
(IWM 392)

who were heading for Bras, on their right, and the 3rd RTR tanks which had started their advance towards Hubert-Folie in battle formation.

"*H Company positioned on the right and F Company on the left followed the 3rd RTR tanks at a distance. The other two companies, E Company (Support Company) and G Company were assigned to the attack on Hubert-Folie.*"

The 2nd Northants Yeomanry CO, Brigadier Churcher, assigned to support the 3rd Mon in capturing Bras, was contacted by Major Bill Close of A Squadron of the 3rd RTR with whom he was in permanent contact for information about enemy strong points, particularly the 88-mms situated to the west.

Major Bill Close recalls: "*As the armour of the 2nd Northants Yeomanry crossed our sector I rode over to their CO's tank to tell them:'For God's sake,*

don't go so far west, you'll be in range of the 88-mm Flak guns located in Ifs, only 2 000 yards away!" I pointed out some smashed up tanks to him; they were still burning, slowly. I assumed he heeded my warning."

To avoid being in the line of fire of the 88-mm Flak guns, Brigadier Churcher told his Squadron Commanders to attack Bras from the northeast. His tankmen had less than 800 yards to cover, but it was across crop fields, right up to the village, and hidden in these crops were the Waffen-SS from III./SS-Pz.Gren.Rgt. 1 in their foxholes armed with Panzerfausts or Mausers with sights.

Suddenly they came under fire then a smoke screen obscured their visibility on their right. Generally the enemy fought hard but when the situation got out of hand they surrendered of their own account.

The CO of the 9./SS-Pz.Gren.Rgt.1, Rudolf Grein, recalls: *"The British artillery barrage lasted all afternoon and was only a prelude to an enemy attack which completely outdid us in materiel. Their tanks advanced. There were two, five, eight, ten then we stopped counting. They approached our foxholes cautiously. We were paralysed with fear. We knew they were going to pulverise us. Those who survived would be captured."*

C Squadron destroyed a Pz.IV and two Paks as it advanced.

In spite of Close's suggestion, the armoured reconnaissance regiment advanced too far west and the 88-mm servers who were waiting for this opportunity, destroyed five of its tanks. It is possible that the losses were caused by the Paks, as the Royal Armoured Corps' logbook suggests. *"While the 3rd Royal Tank Regiment advanced towards Hubert-Folie, A Squadron of the 2nd Northants Yeomanry was sent to the south of Bras to cover it during its*

Above.
From the turret of his tank, Lieutenant-Colonel Silvertop, commanding the 3rd Royal Tank Corps, is ordering his tank crews to advance. Near his tank there are some Churchill AVREs. This shot was taken by Sergeant Laws during the morning of 18 July, while his battalion was approaching the Traorn – Caen railway line under fire from enemy anti-tank guns.
(IWM 3880)

(Continued on page 70)

THE PLAINS OF CAEN
19 JULY 1944

Fall of Bras

Fall of Hubert Folie

Germans positions

British Artillery

Grentheville

To Caen

Bras

2nd N.Y.

H Coy

F Coy

3rd R.T.R.

Soliers

G Coy

2nd F. & F. Yeo

Hubert-Folie

Bourguébus

N 158

To Falaise

0   1 km

A Cromwell I from B Squadron of the 2nd Northants Yeomanry destroyed in the Bras sector. The towing cable can be seen on the front of the tank. It is likely that another tank tried to tow it but had to give up. Equipped with a 6-pound ROQF (57-mm) canon, it was very much outclassed by the Panzers but it outdid them all in mobility with its Meteor aircraft engine. Unfortunately this advantage did not prevent the 2nd Northants Yeomanry from losing all its tanks and from being disbanded at the beginning of August 1944 to be replaced by the 15/16th Hussars.
(Photo : Briois. Coll., M. Dutheil)

Left.
It is surprising to come across a Dukw amongst the Cromwell, Panther and Sherman wrecks in the engagement sector of Bras. However… This amphibious vehicle probably belonged to the Royal Engineers who were ordered to clear the Caen-Vimont railway line situated near Bras and Hubert-Folie of mines.
(Photo: Briois. Coll., M. Dutheil)

Previous page.
The fighting on 19 July 1944 for the capture of Bras and Hubert-Folie.
(from the Rifle Brigade, by Major Hastings)

69

(Continued from page 67)

advance. B Squadron sent a Troop to protect the right flank beyond the main road *(Author's note: Caen-Falaise)*. All this took time and all the time the tanks were in full sight of the enemy who withdrew its Panzers onto some high ground towards the south. As a result, they could keep up continuous fire from the mortars, artillery and long-range self-propelled guns which caused us some losses. One of the Paks which we had signalled as destroyed suddenly came to life again and destroyed three of our tanks at point blank range before being destroyed in turn."

THE "RECCES" RETREAT

Brigadier Churcher realised his mistake too late. Remembering the terrible losses of the day before,

the crews inside their tanks expecting to be blown up at any moment, turned round in complete disorder. Churcher was not even able to reorganise his regiment, so great was their panic.

Major Peck was killed by a shell as he jumped down from his tank. Majors Stancomb and McGillycuddy were both wounded in the head by shrapnel. The crews of two sections returned on foot after their tanks were lost. The section commander's tank was destroyed and another one had its tracks hit by high fragmentation shells. The 23rd Northants Yeomanry only had 23 tanks left out of its initial 61.

As the 2nd Northants Yeomanry tanks were no longer able to invest Bras, the 3rd RTR was unable

to attack Hubert-Folie. Lieutenant-Colonel D.A.H. Silvertop of the 3rd RTR who had been following the whole scene through his binoculars, radioed Brigadier Harvey to warn him about how things had taken a turn for the worse. The latter suggested replacing the 2nd Northants Yeomanry.

It must be remembered that this unit was only a reconnaissance unit, not an armoured regiment although it seems to have been used as one on that day, probably in order to replace the tanks missing from the 29th Armoured Brigade. As a result Silvertop took over the attack on Bras and the armour's task of covering the King's Shropshire Light Infantry (K.S.L.I.) was given to the 2nd Northants Yeomanry.

THE ATTACK ON BRAS

Major Bill Close, commanding A Squadron took an active part in this attack [2]. He recalls: *"As we were progressing, the orders to my tank commanders were brief and clear: "We must take these villages from those heights. The CO recommends avoiding any fighting."*

But in the 3rd Royal Tank Regiment's logbook, there is no mention of the regiment engaging before 16.40 (during the attack on Bras). On the other hand Lieutenant-Colonel Silvertop of the 3rd Royal Tank Regiment received his orders at 14.45 to start attacking Hubert-Folie. It therefore seems likely that Major Close received his orders

---

2 : This account by Major Close raises some questions as to the order of events of that particular day. This officer tells us that after the Typhoons attacked the Panthers he returned to take orders from HQ situated on the railway line at 15.00.

Below.
The motorised infantry from the Rifle Brigade pauses before crossing the Caen-Vimont railway line. Quite a difficult task which made them waste more than an hour. 17-pounder anti-tank gun servers (from the 75th Anti-Tank Regiment) are waiting for their orders.
(IWM 3911)

71

Above.
Two tanks from the 3rd Royal Tank Regiment caught under fire from German artillery on 18 July 1944.
(Photo du Sergeant Laws. IWM 3872)

from his superior a quarter of an hour later as he himself affirmed. What is to be made of the account of the engagement as related by Major Close? As far as we are concerned, we have decided to place his narrative during the attack on Bras to conform to the log book.

"*As we advanced towards Bras I noticed that there were a great deal more enemy tanks set up in excellent positions than we had expected; they were located between the two villages and to the west of Bras. Once again, I took Buck Bite's three tanks with me and tried to go round the village by the west; we found ourselves some 400 yards from the first houses when once again we were subjected to very heavy anti-tank fire from Panthers inside the village, but also from Ifs. Two of Buck's*

tanks were hit immediately and I could see that tanks in B and C Squadrons were burning. I gave Johnny Langdon's Troops the task of trying to advance between the two villages. Once again he bravely led his tanks destroying two Panthers on the way before losing two of his own tanks. I could see several of his crews walking through the wheat fields carrying their wounded with them.

I ordered my men to join us and get under cover, and calling to my radio operator, I asked him to call up the artillery to blast the two villages as quickly as possible. B and C Squadrons fell back onto the railway line which gave them some protection.

I remained with Buck Kite's Sherman which was fitted with a 17-pounder and which was in a "dip" 500 yards to the north of Bras. We were able to engage the Panthers which were trying to get round our flanks. Buck's tank quickly destroyed two of them. My own pointer engaged two self-propelled guns who had been attacking us from the west of Bras.

Once again we were caught by anti-tank fire coming from all directions. It was obvious that the two villages were strongly held and that the presence of the Panthers on the high ground was making our position untenable; I reported to Colonel David (the officer i/c of air-ground coordination) who ordered us to remain where we were and continue to push back the enemy while he tried to get the RAF in to attack the heights.

A short while later, some fighters arrived, went into a dive and attacked the Panthers along our front. Two were destroyed and the others fell back. We remained in our positions rather than advance and lose more tanks. I had five tanks left my own included. B and C Squadrons scarcely had more…"

The veterans of the 8th Motor Battalion recall: "The Motor Platoons remained in their half-tracks until they reached the village and the carriers which went through the wheat fields capturing a large number of prisoners on the way. The leading companies reached the village just behind the 3rd RTR tanks. They jumped down from their vehicles and set about clearing out the houses.

There was strong opposition. The Germans equipped with Panzerfausts jumped out from everywhere. Several Paks revealed themselves."

The 3rd RTR tanks gave the men of the III/SS-Pz. Gren. Rgt. 1 no quarter in their foxholes or trenches. SS-Oberstrumführer Zelinka remembers: *"The point where the enemy broke through was in the sector of the unit just on our left. From there they tried to attack our battalion, attacking on the flank and from behind. Hidden from the English by the crops, most of our company tried to recapture the positions held by the reserve company. Most of the soldiers in my company were in completely open country. Although a great number of enemy tanks were advancing towards our positions, most of the men held fast. Other enemy tanks came up and managed to break into the village from both sides. In turn the infantry arrived and it became impossible for us to break off and rejoin our battalion; at least only a few of us managed to."*

In spite of the young Waffen-SSs' stubborn defence, the crews managed to break up the first resistance points towards 17.00, but their advance was considerably held up by the rubble littering the streets. Sometimes the crews fired one or two shells into the houses in order to advance.

Above.
This young Waffen-SS, perfectly camouflaged in a wheat field is equipped with a Mauser fitted with Zielfernohr 41 sights. This reconstituted scene illustrates the situation of these young soldiers of the SS-Pz.Gren.Rgt. 1 or very well. During Operation Goodwood, their favourite targets were officers and tank commanders.
Reconstitution (Photo: D. L.)

A quarter of an hour later the tanks reaching the centre of the village enabled the motorised infantry to invest the place. H Company attacked on the right and F Company came up in the wake of the tanks to deal with the formidable Waffen-SS soldiers.

On this subject the Rifle Brigade's log book recorded: *"The Germans fought bravely, as we expected. Nevertheless because of the speed with which we entered the village, they had little time to react. Some of them came out of their trenches holding grenades but they were immediately eliminated.*
Inside the village there were still some machine gun positions and snipers but they were reduced to silence. F Company going through the village from

the right arrived just in time to open fire on a group of fifty or so Germans who were trying to escape."

After losing his tank, hit by an 88-mm Flak gun, and part of his crew, Major Bill Close entered the village aboard Sergeant Dale's. About this particular point, he wrote: *"We shot at the fleeing Germans and destroyed two Panthers trying to enter the village from the west. B and C Squadrons - each reduced to two or three tanks - reached the village at the same time; we were obliged to get the walls to collapse on the Germans to force them to surrender. The anti-tank guns were destroyed at point blank range."*

At 18.00, the village had been cleared out and the III./SS-Pz.Gren.Rgt. 1 was considered to have been almost completely annihilated. Almost 300 Waffen-SS had been killed and the others captured; it was written later in the divisional history that

this attack was the model for a combined armour and infantry attack.

The last 3rd RTR tanks withdrew from the village which was still bombarded from time to time. They set themselves up on watch to the north of the village while elements of the 159th Inf. Brig. started moving in.

Worn out by two days' fighting, Lieutenant-Colonel Silvertop radioed Brigadier Harvey for permission to withdraw for 24 hours in order to reorganise the remnants of his battalions. In fact he was given two days for this, and then left for Cussy on 22 July 1944 where he found the village in ruins among which his tanks had to camouflage themselves as best they could.

THE CAPTURE OF HUBERT-FOLIE

Once Bras was taken, the 8th Motor Battalion headed for Hubert-Folie while the 3 Mon came up

to take its place in Bras. Unfortunately, German mortar fire pinned them down for almost two hours, preventing them from rushing to Hubert-Folie. The enemy took advantage of this setback to reinforce their positions. Four British artillery regiments preparing for the attack on Hubert-Folie with a barrage mistook their target and bombarded Bras!

At 18.10, Brigadier Churcher of the 2nd Northants Yeomanry was ordered to attack Hubert-Folie. Ten minutes later he received a counter-order. In the end this hardly enviable mission fell to the 22nd Armoured Brigade. Unconvinced, Churcher asked his crews to remain where they were and wait for the counter-order to be checked. It took the CO twenty minutes before he realised that he had been given the wrong orders. As a result he lost several tanks while waiting for them to be confirmed. After that, the reconnaissance regiment did not have enough tanks to get into battle formation.

The only armoured unit available was the 2nd Fife and Forfar Yeomanry. With its 24 remaining tanks, and preceded by a ten minute artillery barrage, Lieutenant-Colonel Alex Scott's battalion hurried to Hubert-Folie along with G Company of the Rifle Brigade. *"The leading Squadron approached the village before the artillery barrage had stopped. G Company's soldiers, placed on the right, behind the tanks, did not hang around before jumping down from their half-tracks and, as Major Hastings recalls, hit like lightning. In a short time almost 80 SS prisoners were taken. There was not much opposition from the rest of the village except for one Sherman shooting at our Carriers, killing*

Above.
Infantry from H Company of the Rifle Brigade patrol in the ruins of Bras after fighting hard with the Waffen-SS of the 1.SS-Pz.Div. This soldier is equipped with a shoulder belt containing extra cartridges and is also carrying three Piat missiles in their sheaths.
(IWM 3912)

Corporal Isard and wounding several soldiers. The company reproached the tank crews until it was discovered that the Sherman in question had been captured the day before by the Germans. A German who had remained behind in the tank was now firing the on-board machine gun. Once he was located, he was put out of action."

At 20.45, Hubert-Folie was in the hands of the 2nd Fife and Forfar Yeomanry tank crews and G Company. Among the enemy prisoners, the tank crews were able to identify some who had escaped from the fighting in Bras as well as the SS battalion CO.

They were rapidly relieved by the 4th K.S.L.I. of the 159th Infantry Brigade and in coordination with the 23rd Hussars, they then placed themselves in reserve behind the two villages, in case the enemy counter-attacked.

The Rifle Brigade now withdrew for the night to a dip in the ground and rested. In two days it had captured 581 German soldiers and taken or destroyed the following materiel: 27 Nebelwerfers, 5 heavy Paks, 8 trucks, one self-propelled gun and a Volkswagen whose tactical insignia was that of SS-StuG. Abt. 1. The brigade's losses amounted to four wounded officers, seven killed, 75 wounded and two missing. These losses were light considering it had taken part in the capture of these two villages. Credit for this was due to the Rifle Brigade's CO who had worked out an effective plan in spite of the critical situation and had then carried it through with great speed and determination, the Riflemen's qualities.

Opposite page.
Once the sniper has been eliminated the infantrymen advance along one of the streets of Bras. (IWM 3908)

Below.
A 75-mm Pak 40 destroyed by the 3rd Royal Tank Regiment during its attack on Bras. This anti-tank canon was on the edge of a wood near Bourguébus. It belonged to the I. or the II./SS-Pz.Gren.Rgt. 2. By using armour-piercing shells, its servers could fire at a range of up to just more than 1 800 yards. With its high explosive shell its range was 4 912 yards 7 860 m. (IWM 3925)

Above.
These three infantrymen from H Company seen on the previous photograph are taking out the last isolated snipers. This company's losses were light during the taking of Bras. This was not the case when it had had to clear out the wood situated near Hill 112 on 29 June 1944. It had been submitted to mortar and artillery shots which had immobilised it all day. Its company commander, Kenneth MacKenzie had been seriously wounded.
(IWM 3910)

Right.
A Carrier from the 8th Motor Battalion rushing towards Bras. The divisional insignia is quite clearly visible on the mudguard.
(IWM 3873)

BOTTOM LINE

The 29th Armoured Brigade's losses for 19 July were: 4 tanks for the 23rd Hussars, 16 for the 3rd RTR, 8 for the 2nd Fife and Forfar Yeomanry and 37 for the 2nd Northants Yeomanry.

In two days the 11th Armoured Division had lost a total of 191 tanks and 725 officers and men, just to advance 3 miles (6 km).

On 20 July, the 159th Infantry Brigade was replaced by the 7th Canadian Brigade and all the division was withdrawn from the front line. The 3 Mon, the last unit in the 11th Armoured Division to be relieved, fought a serious clash with seven Tigers on its west flank. It destroyed three of them.

During the afternoon, it rained cats and dogs everywhere in the region. The 159th Inf. Div. remained in its positions whilst still protecting the Canadians in case the enemy counter-attacked. Although it encountered considerable difficulties because of the rain, the mud and the artillery barrages, the infantry tried to reform its ranks and did not leave this sector before 22 July, when it moved to Buron, once it had been relieved by the 1st Gordons of the 51st Highland Division.

Two days later the division crossed the Orne and concentrated north of the Caen-Bayeux road while waiting for replacement tanks and men.

Less than ten days after Operation Goodwood, the 11th Armoured, up to strength again, got ready to cross the Orne to take part in a new operation, Bluecoat. This was to be the first big English victory in Normandy in the summer of 1944.

Above.
A 150-mm Nebelwerfer 41 from Werfer Regiment 14. The six barrels of the NbW41 where loaded with explosive shells each weighing nearly 77 lb (35 kg); it could also fire smoke bombs. Its maximum range was 7540 yards (6900 m) and its rate of fire was 6 shells in 10 seconds and three salvoes of 6 shells in five minutes. It was this type of Nebelwerfer which slowed down the 29th Armoured Brigade in front of Grentheville.
(BA 101/I/582/2118/20)

A Cromwell IV from the 2nd Northants Yeomanry destroyed before it reached the heights at Bras. Thanks to this shot taken by M. Briois after the battle, we can see the completely open ground over which the tanks from this unit had to move. The Cromwell IV was easily recognisable by its 75-mm canon fitted with a muzzle brake. Its maximum speed was (52 kph) and it only weighed 28 tonnes. Its crew comprised five men. Apart from its RQQF Mk V 75-mm canon, it was also armed with two 7,92-mm Besa machine guns.
(Photo : Briois. Coll., M. Dutheil)

A lot of losses for few results

It was obvious that Operation Goodwood did not get the results expected. The LXXXVI. A.K.'s defences, set up formidably in depth, had completely prevented the terrain from being exploited in the direction of Falaise and the road remained closed to the British.

THE ONLY GOOD POINT OF THE OPERATION was that it had drawn most of the German armoured divisions onto the 2nd Army's front, of which VIIIth Army Corps was part.

This enabled the 1st Army to deal with Saint-Lô and to gain a new base from which it could launch Operation Cobra leading to the turning point of the war in Normandy.

There are two points which help to explain the failure of *"Goodwood"*. The first was the lack of information about the German defences. If the Air Force had attacked the terrain to the south of the Caen-Vimont railway line, the German artillery concentration would not have been in condition to destroy as many British tanks. In all there were seventy-eight 88-mm Flak guns, 12 heavy AA guns, 194 artillery pieces and

272 Nebelwerfers. One wonders how Ultra could have been so unaware of this "detail" and the presence of the 1.SS-Pz.Div. "Leibstandarte", which sent its Panzers as early as 13.00 against the 29th Armoured Division's three armoured battalions in such a critical situation at that precise moment.

The second point is the lack of artillery support (except for the divisional artillery) which remained to west of the Orne and which was unable to intervene effectively because the guns were out of range, beyond the Caen-Vimont railway line.

In detail there are also some negative points which did not help the VIIIth Army Corps:

A – The element of speed which should have been a major trump card for the armoured battalions was of no use because the front was too narrow,

preventing the tanks from manoeuvring freely.

B – The artillery barrages were carried out according to the terrain and not according to tactical requirements and the enemy positions thus escaped being pounded.

C – The left part of the front line which followed the enemy lines in parallel was only neutralised for a short while by the artillery barrages and air raids. The Panzers and the Strumgeschütze which were not destroyed suddenly reappeared in the battle and inflicted heavy losses on the armoured battalion. Finally almost 20 British tanks were destroyed in the Cagny sector and to the northeast of the woods just to the east of le Prieuré. Smoke screens on this flank, unfortunately wafted back by the wind that was blowing that day, would have been useful. The change

in direction increased the danger on the left flank and to the rear of Frénouville, le Poirier and Cagny.

D – Originally the Guards Armoured Brigade was supposed to watch over the left flank but they were late and this left the flank exposed. Therefore the 29th Armoured Brigade headed for Bras - Hubert-Folie – Soliers and Four without any cover. The situation got worse when the 22nd Armoured Brigade was also late. As a result the two brigades which were committed had no effect on the first day of the offensive.

E – It appears that the brigades were late because on the one hand the battalions had to pass through the 2nd Army's own minefields and on the other hand by the railway lines which turned out to be out-and-out obstacles. These delayed the tanks and other vehicles which could only cross them at specific points.

Above.
This photo taken before operation Goodwood shows a Sherman Firefly with a 17-pounder which enabled it to fight on equal terms against German armour.
(IWM 6751)

Bibliography and documents consulted

- Headquarters Unit 29th Armoured Brigade – War Diary
- 29th Armd. BrigadE – War Diary n°3
- 3rd Royal Tanks – War Diary
- Operations – G Main 11 Armd Div.
- 2nd Northants Yeomanry – War Diary (WO 171/860)
- 13rd RHA Regiment – War Diary
- 75th Anti-Tank Regt. R.A. – War Diary
- 4th KSLI – War Diary
- Herefords (WO 171/1307)
- 2nd Fife and Forfar Yeomanry – War Diary
- 11th Armd. Div. Int. – Summary n°23
- 159th Inf. Brig. – War Diary n°4
- 159th Inf. Brig – Intelligense service – War Diary
- Public record 18 et 19 juillet 1944 (WD 456)
- Royal Armoured Corps Journal. – Vol. X n°2
- 8. R.B. in Operation Goodwood – War Diary
- Akte 21. Pz.Div., Freiburg

Books consulted:

- **The Rifle Brigade,** *Major Hastings,* Aldershot Gale and Polden Ltd, 1950.
- **From the Desert to the Baltic,** *Major-General Pip Roberts,* W. Kimber Pub.
- **History f the South Wales Borderers,** *Major J.J. How,* Hughes and son, 1954.
- **Soldier in the saddle,** *Monkey Blacker,* Burke London Publishing.
- **The story of the 23rd Hussars,** *members of this unit's association.*
- **A view from the Turret,** *Major Bill Close,* Dell and Bredon Publishing.
- **Taurus pursuant, a History of 11th Armoured Division,** *Association.*
- **The Fife and Forfar Yeomanry,** *R.J.B. Sellar,* W. Blackwood and son.
- **Panzer Bait,** *William Moore-Leo Cooper,* 1991.
- **The proud trooper,** *Major W. Steel,* Brownlee-Collins.
- **The History of 4th HSLI,** *Lieutenant-Commander P.K. Kemp,* Wilding and Son Ltd, 1955.
- **The 4th KSLI in Normandy,** *Major Thornburn,* 1990.
- **The charge of the Bull,** *Jean Brisset,* Bates Books 1989.
- **Manu Forth,** *Lieutenant-Colonel Hill,* Allan Sutton Publishing.
- **The Devil's own,** *Major D.M. Hatton,* J.A. Allen Publishing, 1992.
- **Monkey Business,** *General Sir Cecil Blacker,* Quiller Press London.
- **45 Tiger en Normandie,** *Lodieu Didier,* Ysec Editions.
- **Goodwood,** *P. Wirton et G. Bernage,* Heimdal.
- **The Leibstandarte IV/1,** *R. Lehman et R. Tieman,* J.J. Fedsorowicz Publishing Inc.

Thanks

I should like to express my gratitude particularly to Simon Trew, military historian of the Sandhurst Military Academy, England, who allowed me to make use of an extraordinary ensemble of documents relating to operation *"Goodwood"*. I should also like to thank Thierry Guilbert. A big thanks to Jean-Marie Mongin and Denis Gandilhon who had faith in the making of this book, as well as to Philippe Charbonnier, always there when help is needed.

This book has been realised by Denis Gandilhon.
Conception, make-up and realisation by Gil Bourdeaux and Matthieu Pleissinger.

Histoire & Collections

SA au capital de 182 938,82 €

5, avenue de la République
F-75541 Paris Cédex 11

Tel: +33-1 40 21 18 20 / Fax: +33-1 47 00 51 11
w w w . h i s t o i r e e t c o l l e c t i o n s . f r

This book has been designed, typed, laid-out and processed by *Histoire & Collections* and *"le Studio Graphique A & C"* on fully integrated computer equipment.

Color separation: *Studio A&C*

Print by Elkar, Spain, EEC.
May 2008